in GOD'S *company*
Christian Giants
of Business

Peter Lupson

© Peter Lupson 2019
First printed 2019
Reprinted 2020
Reprinted 2021

ISBN 978-1-84625-658-5

British Library Cataloguing in Publication Data available

Unless otherwise indicated, Scripture quotations are from the New King James
Version (NKJV) ®. Copyright © 1982 by Thomas Nelson, Inc. Used by permission.
All rights reserved.

Published by Day One Publications
Ryelands Road, Leominster, HR6 8NZ
☎ 01568 613 740
email—sales@dayone.co.uk
web site—www.dayone.co.uk

Original cover design by Benjamin Hughes
Cover illustration by Kathryn Chedgzoy
Printed by 4edge Limited

For my son, Mike, who gave me the idea.
Also for my grandchildren Daniel, Emily, Olivia
and Thomas.

Endorsements

Contents

Acknowledgements

One of the greatest pleasures of writing a book is the sheer joy of discovery. I have learned so much about these seven remarkable entrepreneurs and the times and places in which they lived and worked. I am immensely grateful, therefore, to the many people and organizations who have helped me in significant ways with the chapter against which I have listed their names:

William Colgate

John and Julie Dinnis, Filston Hall Farm, Shoreham, Kent

Amanda Hughes, Maryland Department, Enoch Pratt Free Library, Baltimore

Rev. Charlie Ingram, Minister, Bessels Green Baptist Church, Kent

Nancy Kandoian, Map Division, Stephen A. Schwarzman Building, New York Public Library

Professor David Killingray, President, Sevenoaks Historical Society, Kent

Irma and Paul Milstein Division, Stephen A. Schwarzman Building, New York Public Library

Francis P. O'Neill, Reference Librarian, Maryland Historical Society

Scott Rubin, Visitor Services Manager, Maryland Historical Society, Baltimore

Daphne Ship, Archivist, Bessels Green Baptist Church, Kent

Lara Westwood, Special Projects Archivist, Maryland Historical Society, Baltimore

Thomas Cook

Rev. Nicholas Cook, Minister, Market Harborough Baptist Church

Jess Jenkins, Archivist, Record Office for Leicestershire, Leicester and Rutland, Wigston Magna

Acknowledgements

Alison Mott, Loughborough History and Heritage Network, Loughborough University

Ian Porter, Loughborough Library Local Studies

Gillian Pritchard, Loughborough Library Local Studies

Paul Smith, Company Archivist, Thomas Cook UK & Ireland

Douglas Wooldridge, Archivist, Market Harborough Baptist Church and also Archivist, East Midland Baptist Association, Nottingham

Henry Crowell

Government Publications Department, Chicago Public Library

Kevin Gray, Reference Librarian, Reed Memorial Library, Ravenna, Ohio

Terry Metter, Center for Local & Global History, Cleveland Public Library, Ohio

Danilo Milich, Center for Local & Global History, Cleveland Public Library, Ohio

Jamie S. Pawlack, Destination Cleveland, Ohio

Rachel Ramirez, Curator, Winnetka Historical Society, Chicago

Reference Desk, Winnetka-Northfield Public Library District, Chicago

Lisa Sanchez, Center for Local & Global History, Cleveland Public Library, Ohio

Corie Zylstra, Crowell Library Archives, Moody Bible Institute, Chicago

William Hartley

Christine Bradley, Reference and Local Studies Librarian, Colne Library, Lancashire

Dr David France, President, Everton FC Heritage Society

Roger Hull, Research Officer, Record Office, Central Library, Liverpool

Sue Kauffman, Libraries Archives, Liverpool Record Office

Debbie Kershaw, Finance and HR Administrator, St Mark's Medical Centre, Southport

Canon Dr Jon Richardson, Former Diocesan Director of Education, Liverpool

Acknowledgements

Billy Smith, Archivist, Everton FC Heritage Society, Liverpool

Darran Ward, Library Service, Colne Library, Lancashire

Henry Heinz

Jenny Benford, Director of Programming, The Homewood Cemetery Historical Fund, Pittsburgh

Dr Randy Bush, Senior Pastor, East Liberty Presbyterian Church, Pittsburgh

Scott Hersberger, Director, Tourism Services, Visit Pittsburgh

Marilyn Holt, Pennsylvania Department, Carnegie Library of Pittsburgh

Nancy Reynolds, Welcome Center Manager, Pittsburgh Information

Louise Sturgess, Executive Director, Pittsburgh History & Landmarks Foundation

James Kraft

E-Mail Reference Team, Ask a Librarian, Chicago Public Library

David Feiler, Business Manager, North Shore Baptist Church, Chicago

Sean Fleming, Adult Services Librarian, Fort Erie Public Library, Ontario, Canada

Pastor Doug Harris, North Shore Baptist Church, Chicago

Jude Scott, Curator, Collections, Conservation and Research, Fort Erie Museum and Cultural Services, Ontario, Canada

Anthony Rossi

Pastor Clark Edwards, First United Methodist Church, Bradenton, Florida

Terri Hill, Director of Connections, Calvary Baptist Church, Bradenton, Florida

Ralph Nicosia, Former Vice-President and member of the Board of Directors, Tropicana Products Inc., Bradenton, Florida

Pastor Rick Speece, Calvary Baptist Church, Bradenton, Florida

Laura Tjaden, Comment Moderator, Visit Florida, Tallahassee

The following books, written by a family member of the respective entrepreneur, provided particularly valuable insights:

Acknowledgements

Bittersweet: The Story of Hartley's Jam by Nicholas Hartley (great-grandson of Sir William Hartley). Stroud: Amberley Publishing, 2011.

Anthony T. Rossi: Christian and Entrepreneur by Sanna Barlow Rossi (wife of Anthony T. Rossi). Downers Grove, IL: InterVarsity Press, 1986.

I am very grateful to my son Mike for not only giving me the idea for the book but also for carefully editing each chapter as soon as I had written it. His many astute observations removed inconsistencies and other blemishes from my early drafts.

I would also like to thank my daughter Karen for the title and for her enthusiastic support for the project.

Finally, many thanks to Richard Worsley, Headteacher, Christian Fellowship School, Liverpool, for reading each chapter and for his feedback and constant encouragement.

Introduction

'Business is business!' In the fierce white heat of competition, this statement declares that personal feelings or moral considerations can be suspended in the pursuit of profit. As in love and war, 'All's fair' in business. Or is it?

Not according to the seven giants of business who are the subjects of this book. Each of them—world leaders in their field—built empires worth billions but did so with absolute integrity, caring about the quality of their products, service to their customers and the treatment of their employees. There were no shady dealings.

But they didn't have it easy. On their way to staggering success they endured scepticism and ridicule, bitter opposition and, in some cases, terrible personal tragedy. They all suffered severe financial reverses and some even knew the stigma of bankruptcy. Yet, despite devastating setbacks, the word 'impossible' never featured in their vocabulary. Nor did they resort to moral shortcuts to achieve their aims, not even in the worst of times.

What was the secret of their success? These brilliant businessmen publicly acknowledged that they drew the courage, strength and wisdom to turn difficulties into opportunities and disasters into triumphs from their personal relationship with Jesus Christ. In response to their prayers, they knew He would guide them in all their decision-making, in good times and in bad.

All of us, whether in business or not, can identify with some of the pressures these men endured and the pain they suffered. But this is a book about triumph. Its purpose is to let them show us, through the lives they lived and the things they said, how Christ inspired and sustained them. For, as one of them wrote: 'This is the secret of all true success; the consecration of ourselves to Him who loved us and laid down His life for us.'

WILLIAM COLGATE
and the birth of the brand

One night in March 1795, twelve-year-old William Colgate and his family were awakened by the sound of frantic knocking on their farmhouse door. It was a messenger from Prime Minister William Pitt urging them to flee from England. William's father, a friend of Pitt, had fallen foul of the king and now faced imprisonment, possibly even death. Alerted to the danger, the Colgates made immediate plans to sail to America and safety.

This was the incredible start of a chain of events that was to lead to William Colgate establishing a brand that became world-famous first for the manufacture of soap then of toothpaste.

The Colgate family

William was one of eleven children—five boys and six girls—born to Robert and Sarah Colgate. Robert was farming in Hollingbourne, Kent, when William was born there on 25 January 1783. Six years later the family moved some twenty-five miles to Shoreham, Kent, where Robert had bought Filston Hall farm. The sixteenth-century farmhouse in which the family lived is still standing.

The Colgates were a devout Baptist family who worshipped in what is now called The Old Meeting House in the village of Bessels Green near Sevenoaks. It was opened in 1716 and the original building continues to be a place of worship, although no longer Baptist. Robert's father, grandfather and brother had all served as deacons there at different times. Robert himself was a faithful member of the church, regularly attending services with his family. Many of William's relatives lie buried in the churchyard.

The family in danger

As well as firm religious beliefs, Robert held deep political convictions.

Chapter 1

It was these that got him into serious trouble. Believing passionately in political and religious freedom, he had welcomed the overthrow of the king and the aristocracy in the French Revolution of 1789 and he had been an outspoken supporter of the struggle of the thirteen American colonies to break free from British rule and form a new independent republic, the United States of America. He had made no secret of the fact that he regarded the American general, George Washington, as a hero. Each day he had followed the progress of the colonists on a map on his table. If he heard they had won a battle, he would shout for joy.

These were extremely dangerous views and Robert did not hold back from publicly proclaiming them in Sevenoaks at the after-market dinners in the town's inns. But he clearly crossed the line when he openly expressed contempt for King George III, arousing suspicion that he might be involved in a plot against him. As a result, his name was placed at the top of a list of the seven most dangerous men in England. The charge was treason and the punishment imprisonment, deportation or even death. It could only be a matter of time before he was arrested.

Fortunately he was a lifelong friend of William Pitt, who had become Prime Minister at only twenty-four, still the youngest in British history. Whatever Pitt's attitude towards Robert's views, he remained his faithful friend. Despite the risk to himself, he was not prepared to let Robert fall into the king's hands. Hearing that an arrest was imminent, Pitt promptly sent his brother-in-law, Lord Stanhope, to ride at top speed to Filston Hall farm to warn the Colgates of the impending danger. As Prime Minister, he could use his powers to delay the inevitable arrest but he made it clear to Robert he could hold back the authorities for no more than a few days. The family had to get out of England as quickly as possible.

Escape to America
Robert wasted no time in taking Pitt's advice and when he learned that a ship, the *Eliza*, was shortly due to sail from Gravesend for Baltimore in America, he arranged to be on it with his wife Sarah, their six children and a few relatives. But he had to act fast. He couldn't start a new life in another country without money and he could only raise this from the quick sale of his assets. Although hated by the king, Robert was loved by the ordinary folk of the district and the money poured in.

With cash in hand the Colgates set off for Gravesend twelve miles away. Sarah travelled with five of the children by stagecoach while Robert and William rode on horseback. There was a huge turnout of friends and neighbours at the farm to see them off and for several miles along the road well-wishers, many in tears, cheered them and scattered flowers in front of them. Robert was overcome with emotion and pulled his cap down over his eyes to conceal his tears. It hurt to leave behind so many good friends and loyal supporters.

He boarded the *Eliza* and left the shores of England with a heavy heart. Two months later, on 28 May 1795, the Colgates arrived in Baltimore in Maryland. Although it had been painful to leave their homeland, it proved to be the right decision. Almost immediately after the *Eliza* had sailed three of the men on the king's wanted list were arrested and imprisoned. Robert and his family had escaped just in time.

Early struggles in the New World

Initially things went well in their new life. Robert bought a farm in beautiful countryside bordering the Deer Creek Valley near Darlington, north-east of Baltimore. The family were very happy there. William, in particular, was in his element swimming, fishing and hunting. It was during this settled period that his brothers John and George were born. But after only two years this happy time came to an abrupt end when, out of the blue, a claimant to the farm and land appeared. To Robert's utter dismay, he was informed that his deed of purchase was not valid. He had been misled when the original documentation was drawn up. No longer legally entitled to live on the farm, the family had to leave.

Robert was faced with a huge financial crisis. At one stroke most of his assets were wiped out but thankfully he had just enough left to be able to buy another farm in the neighbouring state of West Virginia. But why leave Maryland for a farm in West Virginia? Because there was coal in the land and Robert was confident he could mine and sell it.

He worked long, hard hours to try to make a success of his coal business but sadly, in 1800 after three years of continual struggle, the venture ended in failure. He was left with no option but to abandon rural life and look for employment in Baltimore. It was another terrible blow but this latest downturn in Robert's fortunes proved to be a black cloud with a silver lining. It was to set his son William directly on a path that would lead to unimaginable fame and fortune.

Finding work with a soap- and candle-maker

Robert found work with a soap- and candle-maker, Ralph Mather, who needed help in his workshop. Mather also took on seventeen-year-old William as an apprentice. Although the nature of Robert's work was very different from farming, he quickly settled into it. Mather found him to be reliable, conscientious and efficient and before long invited him into partnership in the business. Robert accepted.

Like his father, William had to adjust to a completely new way of life. Whereas work on a farm was varied, work as an apprentice soap-maker was repetitive and monotonous. William spent most of his time boiling and stirring soap in large kettles, pouring the soap into cooling moulds, then helping to pack it into boxes and jars ready for sale. But surprisingly for a young man who had known only the wide open spaces of country life, he took the cramped, hot environment of the workshop in his stride and developed a genuine passion for the work.

First business venture

Robert enjoyed a good relationship with Mather and their business did well. The family had settled in a pleasant location on Hampstead Hill (now part of Patterson Park) and it seemed as if the Colgates would make Baltimore their permanent home. But in 1802 things changed. Aware that his widowed sister was struggling to bring up her five young children some two hundred miles away in the village of Sing Sing (now Ossining) in New York State, Robert felt strongly that he and his family should move closer to her. When a small farm in her locality became available, he jumped at the chance to buy it. After two years making soap and candles, he was to become a farmer again. By this time William was nineteen and old enough to look after himself. With his steady employment in Mather's workshop it was agreed that he should remain in Baltimore.

William was happy with this arrangement as he liked Mather and enjoyed working for him. However, within a short time he grew restless. He was convinced he had learned enough about soap- and candle-making to set up in business on his own in Baltimore. The financial support of an aunt made it possible for him to take this step. Armed with youthful enthusiasm and a firm belief in his abilities, he threw all his energies into the new enterprise. But it wasn't enough. Despite his best efforts the business failed within a year.

The canal boat captain

Dejected and discouraged, William took a walk along a canal towpath to try to clear his head. He didn't know what to do next. Lost in thought, he suddenly caught sight of a former neighbour on the towpath. It was a canal boat captain. The two started talking. William explained that his soap- and candle-making business had just collapsed. He had failed in the only trade he knew and now felt lost. The captain, a devout Christian, offered to pray for him there and then. William readily agreed.

After praying for William, the captain gave him advice that was to prove prophetic:

> Someone will soon be the leading soap-maker in New York. It can be you as well as anyone. I hope it may. Be a good man; give your heart to Christ; give the Lord all that belongs to Him of every dollar you earn; make an honest soap; give a full pound; and I am certain you will be a prosperous and rich man.

The captain's words had a profound effect on William. They made him think deeply about his future and he gradually became convinced that, despite the disappointment of his failed business venture, he should not give up the trade he had grown to love. The idea of going to New York also made perfectly good sense. With a population much larger than Baltimore's, it offered far greater business opportunities. He felt this was the place to start again. He would take the captain's advice and 'make an honest soap' and 'give a full pound' in that city.

'An honest soap' and 'a full pound'

What did the captain mean by those words? He was referring to two kinds of dishonest practice prevalent at the time. The first concerned the composition of the soap itself. Ordinary soap was made from low-grade oils combined with dripping (solidified animal fat produced after cooking meat). It was coarse and very rough on the hands. A much gentler soap was produced from pure olive oil imported from Castile in Spain but it was a luxury only the rich could afford. To make an easy profit, disreputable manufacturers passed off as Castile soap a product in which low-grade oils were combined with only a small amount of pure olive oil. Starch was often added as a filler to reduce the amount of oil needed.

The second form of cheating was in the weight of the soap. It was weighed by the pound and often boxes were packed with less than the full measure. When the captain urged William always to 'give a full pound' he had in mind unscrupulous merchants who did not do this.

Arrival in New York City

In 1803, William, aged twenty, left Baltimore for New York City. The failure of his business had taught him humility. He realized he didn't know as much about soap-making as he thought. Having spent only two years in Ralph Mather's small workshop, he recognized that he needed the experience of working in a much larger factory before being ready to strike out on his own again.

On arrival in New York he immediately started to look for work with a soap manufacturer. After several hours of searching he came across John Slidell's factory at 50 Broadway in Manhattan and knew at once that this was what he was looking for. He went in to enquire about work. Slidell himself spoke to him and told him there were no vacancies in the factory although a position was available in the office as a clerk's assistant. William firmly but politely declined, saying he was only interested in learning as much as he could about the soap manufacturing process. The role of assistant clerk would not meet his needs. Slidell was so impressed by the young man's determination and open, honest face that he decided he would, after all, find work for him in the factory. He told his foreman: 'Give this young man work. Show him everything about the business. He will be of great service to you.'

William was a fast learner. He became expert at his work and before long was transferred from manufacturing to sales to further his understanding of the wider aspects of the business. He excelled at this too and was promoted to business manager. By the age of twenty-three, after three years at Slidell's, he felt he had acquired enough experience and expertise to set up on his own and not repeat the mistakes of his earlier venture.

Launch of The Colgate Company

The first step was to find suitable premises in a convenient location that could accommodate a workshop, a store and living quarters. He found what he needed at 6 Dutch Street near Broadway. The building had two levels. The ground floor had sufficient space for a workshop and store while the floor above provided reasonable living quarters. With a proper base from which to operate, William launched The Colgate Company in 1806.

It was initially a one-man operation. He spent long hours of hard work boiling and stirring soap, often deep into the night. He also had to run the store. It was a lonely life and it prompted him to invite his twenty-two-year-old sister Maria to join him as his housekeeper. Maria, who had been helping to look after the younger children on the family farm, was excited at the prospect of living in New York City. She was allowed to join her brother.

William quickly gained a reputation for honesty and outstanding service. As a result, the business grew rapidly in its first year. Many years later, in an address to an audience of students, he explained the reason for his success. The secret, he said, was customer care, and he gave the following example.

On the day the store opened a man came in to buy a two-pound bar of soap. William asked where he wanted it delivered. The customer said his house was too far for convenient delivery and he would take it himself, but William insisted that it would be no trouble. He closed his store an hour early and took the soap to the man's home. He told the students: 'The delivery of this cake of soap may have cost me double my profit on that first sale but, young gentlemen, I won a good customer and I have kept him ever since.'

Under pressure

During William's first year in business his father found himself in deep financial trouble. Following a period in Ossining, Robert was appointed manager of a large farm in Mamaroneck. It turned out to be a disaster. His working relationship with the owner was strained and after two years it finally broke down. Despite an upturn in the farm's fortunes since Robert had taken over, the owner was not satisfied and unjustly accused Robert of poor productivity and dishonesty. He ordered him off the farm and took out a lawsuit against him. Legal costs forced Robert to sell his remaining assets and he was left with no means of supporting himself and his family.

William immediately came to the family's aid, renting a property for them in Charlton, near Saratoga Springs. But it was a struggle for him. His fledgling business, although growing, was not yet generating enough income for him to shoulder these extra costs. To ease the burden, he took on a partner, Francis Smith, and on 1 January 1807 the company changed its name to Smith and Colgate.

From bitterness to faith

The Mamaroneck affair left a bitter taste in William's mouth. He felt his father had already suffered enough with expulsion from England and the unfair loss of the farm in Maryland. The present crisis was one too many and William felt deep resentment towards the person he held responsible for plunging Robert into poverty. But during 1807 he was profoundly disturbed by a sudden illness which made him believe he was dying. The shock of this led to a drastic change in the way he saw himself. Convinced he was close to death, he became conscious of a deep sense of his sinful nature and felt the full impact of Christ's words: 'I tell you the truth, no-one can enter the kingdom of God unless he is born of water and the Spirit. Flesh gives birth to flesh, but the Spirit gives birth to spirit. You should not be surprised at my saying, "You must be born again"' (John 3:5–7, NIV 1984).

Despite regular church attendance, William knew that he had not been 'born of the Spirit' because his heart was full of bitterness. How could he possibly expect to receive God's forgiveness and enter heaven when he himself was so unforgiving? He cried out to God:

> God and Father of mercy, . . . I prostrate myself at thy throne, beseeching thee to hear my prayer . . . correct and subdue in me all inordinate desires and unholy attachments; impress thy law on my soul that it may establish my principles and influence my behaviour, that both the thoughts of my heart and tenor of my life may be such as become a Christian. . . . Engrave upon my mind a sense of the character I should maintain.

As the canal boat captain had urged, William gave his 'heart to Christ'. As a result he came out of the illness a changed man and knew that he had—to use his own words—'experienced the new birth'.

As his sister Maria, too, had had a profound conversion experience, they gratefully acknowledged their debt to 'our dear Lord' who had 'given us a new heart and put a new spirit within us'.

From now on William's relationship with Christ became the foremost priority in his life. It stamped his character and shaped his attitude towards everything he did.

The horns of a dilemma

But William's resolve to put Christ first was soon put to the test. Having become a Christian, he now wanted to commit to a church. Maria felt likewise. Their initial impulse was to remain at the church they were already attending. William readily admitted there was the added attraction of the good business connections he could make there:

> There were a number of wealthy and respectable merchants [in that church] who seemed cordially to salute me. . . . I had just commenced business and by their influence and kindness I could expect my prosperity to be furthered. Like young expectants generally, I could but calculate that success in my business would be advanced by businessmen of wealth. . . . To unite with this church there appeared every inducement and at this determination my sister and I arrived without a thought of looking further.

Before deciding to commit themselves, they wrote to their parents to ask their advice. Robert promptly replied. He was clearly delighted at their firm intention to be good Christians: 'The seriousness of your minds, a sense of your duty toward God, and the desire you manifest to live in the practice of piety are truly gratifying to your mother and me.' However, with regard to William's anticipated business advantages, he was straight to the point: 'Take great care that your motive in joining any society is not of an unworthy nature, in order to form worldly connections.'

Robert had a further reservation. He was concerned that the church they were attending baptized infants, a practice with which he did not agree. He believed that baptism should be reserved exclusively for those old enough to understand what it meant. However, having always encouraged his children to think for themselves, he did not push the point, stating: 'What I have communicated to you on the subject of religion has been with care not to influence your mind with bigotry.' All he asked was that they should closely examine what the Bible said about baptism and 'judge impartially'.

Challenged by their father's misgivings, William and Maria made a close study of relevant Bible passages and also discussed the subject in depth with the minister of the church they were attending. After careful consideration, they reached the same understanding as their father. They decided, therefore, to commit to Gold Street Baptist Church in New York City where they were duly baptized by the pastor in February 1808. William explained what a difficult decision it had been to change their church:

> After much reflection we came to the conclusion that . . . we must be Baptists. Yet to do so, in our estimation then, we should have to leave good preaching for poor; in place of uniting with a respectable [group of] people we should unite with one accounted by the world as ignorant and low in life. We must thus sacrifice connections which promised happiness and a good prospect for aiding us in life; and thus viewing fully our duty and our situation, we came to the hard conclusion that duty we must do.

William needn't have worried that switching to the Gold Street church might adversely affect his business. By 1809 his company was making such good profits that he could afford to buy Robert a farm in Andes, New York State. It gave Robert a new lease of life. Free from financial worries, he enjoyed working on the farm, among other things learning how to make potash, an essential ingredient in soap-making. He supplied William's factory with large quantities of it. After seventeen happy years on the farm, Robert died on 26 July 1826 aged sixty-seven. He was buried in Andes Cemetery. He had lived long enough to see William's remarkable success as a businessman and his growth to maturity as a Christian.

The stolen Bible

At Gold Street William always kept a Bible permanently in his pew for use in the services. One Sunday morning it was missing and he realized it had been stolen. Rather than feeling anger towards the thief, he was immediately sympathetic, saying: 'What a pity any should so need a Bible as to steal it!'

It troubled him that someone should be so poor as to need to resort to theft to acquire one. He brought his concern to the attention of his fellow church members and other Christian friends and convinced them that a society should be formed for the purpose of providing free Bibles for the poor. His proposal was enthusiastically embraced and as a result the Young

Men's Bible Society of New York was founded on 11 February 1809. It was only the second organization in the United States to provide free Bibles, the first having been formed in Philadelphia two months previously.

Marriage to Mary Gilbert

Despite the demands of his business, William always found time to visit Robert and the family in Andes. On one of these visits he was introduced to Mary Gilbert, the daughter of a prosperous farmer who was one of Robert's neighbours.

The Gilberts were also originally from England. Mary was born in London on Christmas Day 1788 and was just eight years old when her family came to America. Her father's wealth ensured that she enjoyed a very comfortable upbringing and received a good education. She was a particularly gifted artist. After a period of courtship, William and Mary were married at Gold Street Baptist Church on 23 April 1811. William was twenty-eight, Mary twenty-three.

Having grown up in relative luxury, Mary would have found their first married home in Water Street not far from William's works very modest in stark contrast to her grand home in the country. Nevertheless, she embraced the change wholeheartedly and it was the start of a very happy forty-four-year marriage. They were of one mind, sharing the same religious convictions and the same values. Soon after their wedding, they joined the Oliver Street Baptist Church in New York City where William was appointed a deacon. He was known for the rest of his life as Deacon Colgate.

Their first child, Robert, named after William's father, was born on 26 January 1812. They were to have eight more children—five sons and three daughters.

Buying out Francis Smith

By 1813 William was in a position to buy Francis Smith out. As part of the deal it was agreed that Smith would not establish a soap- and candle-making business of his own in New York City within the next three years. He honoured the agreement and did not, in fact, set up on his own in that city until twenty years later. With Smith's departure, William took on his brother Bowles as his new partner and the company changed its name to William Colgate & Company.

Chapter 1

In tandem with the development of his business, William was also tireless in Christian work. Having helped form a Bible society in New York City, he became actively involved in the provision of free Bibles at national level. In 1816 he played a key role in the merger of thirty-one societies to form the American Bible Society and was appointed to its Board of Managers. He later held positions of great responsibility in other national Bible societies until his death.

Leading soap manufacturer in America

Just as William's involvement in Christian work had extended beyond New York, so too his business was breaking new ground. By 1817, as a result of their reputation for integrity, quality and excellent customer service, William and Bowles had established the company as the leading soap manufacturer in America, producing more than all the others combined. They now began to look further afield. Their first ever newspaper advertisement appeared that year and contained a significant pointer to the pair's expanding horizons: 'Orders for exportation executed on the shortest notice.'

With business booming, the factory couldn't keep up with demand. The whole of Dutch Street was regularly blocked with carts queuing to collect their orders and they would frequently overflow into Fulton Street, sometimes even as far as Broadway. In order to increase capacity the factory was enlarged by incorporating 4 and 8 Dutch Street. Even this proved inadequate and two additional buildings were rented on William Street. Again, growth outstripped their current facilities and further property had to be acquired at 53 and 55 John Street.

William never took the company's growth for granted. He saw it as a blessing from God and was ever mindful of the words of the canal boat captain: 'Give the Lord all that belongs to Him of every dollar you earn.' He took these words to heart, faithfully setting aside one-tenth of his earnings for God's work. As his business grew and prospered he increased the amount proportionately, eventually giving 50 per cent of his income.

Support for student training

One of William's abiding passions was the education and preparation of young men for Christian ministry, a cause to which he devoted huge amounts of time and money. He was involved from the very beginning with initiatives that worked towards this end.

When the Baptist Education Society of the State of New York was granted a charter in 1819 to establish a theological school in Hamilton (some two hundred miles from New York City), William gave the scheme his full support. In May 1820 the school opened under the name of Hamilton Literary and Theological Institution.

William was totally committed to the work of the school, serving as a member of its Board of Trustees for many years. He gave continual financial support which included buying groceries for the boarding house, providing books, paying professors' salaries and endowing scholarships. His wife Mary also had a great love for the school and played an active part in helping impoverished students. She was a member of the Female Society of New York City, a Christian organization formed to provide scholarships, food and clothing for the poorest students. These kind women were looked upon by the students as their adopted mothers.

Passion for missionary work

Central to all William's Christian activities was his firm belief in the gospel message—that Jesus sets people free from sin and invites them to enjoy a personal relationship with Him. He considered it a matter of the utmost importance to make this message known: 'We believe there is nothing in the whole range of human enterprise that can be compared in magnitude or importance with the gospel for improving and ameliorating the condition of mankind, and that it is the distinguishing glory of our churches to direct their energies primarily to its promotion.'

He was active in a number of organizations that promoted this message. In 1829 he was elected to the Board of Managers of the Baptists' General Missionary Convention which he served for twenty-three years. That same year he was made a life member of the Baptist Missionary Convention of the State of New York, later becoming its vice-president. In 1832 he was appointed treasurer of the American Baptist Home Mission Society and was later elected to its Board of Managers. He was also an honorary life manager of the Baptist Tract Society which published literature promoting the Christian faith. He gave these organizations generous financial support but he was also mindful of the needs of individual missionaries, not only helping them financially but also making his home available to them as a base before leaving for, or when returning from, periods of service abroad.

Rescuing an ailing church

Close to where William and Mary worshipped in Oliver Street stood Mulberry Street Baptist Church, a grand building with a seating capacity of 1,500. It was one of the largest churches in New York City but for some years the congregation had been dwindling. Falling numbers meant an ever-decreasing income and by 1838 the church's finances were in a perilous state. Maintenance costs and mortgage payments could not be met and the trustees had no option but to put the building up for sale.

William saw this as an exciting opportunity. His vision was to combine this dwindling congregation with other struggling local congregations into a single vibrant church in the spacious Mulberry Street building. The Oliver Street Church shared his vision, acquired the building and carried out the necessary repairs to make it a fitting place of worship. William himself donated much of the capital for the project. By the following year all work had been completed and the new church, now called the Tabernacle Baptist Church, opened its doors with some 350 members. William was appointed a deacon and served the church for the rest of his life. Its first pastor, William Wallace Everts, started his ministry in October 1839.

The impact of Jacob Knapp

In the winter of 1838–39, shortly before the formation of the Tabernacle Church, the nationally renowned evangelist Rev. Jacob Knapp held a series of outreach meetings in Baltimore. William had attended some of these and was so conscious of God's presence in them that he proposed that Knapp should be invited to hold similar meetings at the Tabernacle Church.

Knapp was a dynamic evangelist who thundered against sin yet never indulged in mere emotionalism. His sermons were full of homely illustrations supported by biblical references and clear logic. Outwardly serious, even stern, he was blessed with a sharp sense of humour and could make an entire congregation laugh whenever he pleased, but could just as easily silence them merely by raising his finger.

Knapp accepted the Tabernacle Church's invitation and early in 1840 spent nine consecutive weeks speaking there, staying at William's home during that time. The building couldn't hold the huge crowds that flocked there each evening. There was enough room for two thousand, but thousands more could not get in.

The impact of the meetings was phenomenal. The *New York Herald* filled its pages with reports of Knapp's sermons and the amazing response to them. It was estimated that about two thousand were converted. Some five hundred of the converts immediately joined the Tabernacle Church while hundreds more joined other churches in the city.

One of the most active workers throughout the campaign was William himself. He was always at the front door warmly welcoming visitors as they entered. After the meetings he was always available to talk to anyone who wanted to know more about the Christian faith. He even hired extra help in his office in Dutch Street so that he could make time to visit enquirers in their homes and encourage them. Knowing that many new converts abandoned their good intentions once their initial enthusiasm had worn off, William helped arrange a system of neighbourhood prayer meetings for them in various homes in the city. By this means large numbers continued steadily on in their Christian lives. The Tabernacle Church flourished and in 1850 a new building was erected on Second Avenue.

The organ controversy

William had a huge influence at the Tabernacle. In the churches of the day it was usual to sing without instrumental accompaniment because musical instruments were associated with secular entertainment and therefore considered unsuitable for church worship. In fact, only one Baptist church in the whole of New York City had an organ. But William loved music and believed the addition of an organ would greatly enhance the services of the Tabernacle. It was a controversial issue because most of the members were strongly opposed to the idea. William was sensitive to their feelings and came up with an ingenious compromise. He offered to have an organ brought into the church at his own expense and music played on a Saturday evening when everyone would be invited to listen. If it was still felt to be unsuitable for services, he would promptly have it removed.

There was a huge turnout the evening it arrived. The opening hymn was 'Praise God from Whom All Blessings Flow'. It was sung by a choir of sixty to the accompaniment of the organ. The effect was electrifying. The melodious combination of organ and voices enraptured the congregation and they sang their hearts out with the choir the whole evening. It was used at the service the very next morning and once again lifted the singing to new heights. It was never removed.

The peacemaker

William's tact and sensitivity were evident in other ways too. A woman who had been the mistress of a well-known public figure became ashamed of the life she had been leading. She found faith in Christ and left her old life behind. Wanting to join a church, she applied to become a member of the Tabernacle but there was reluctance on the part of some of the congregation to accept her without a period of probation. They wanted to be sure she really had changed. This caused a rift with those who felt she should be accepted unconditionally. It was decided to put the matter to a vote but before it went ahead, William put the doubters firmly in their place with delightful irony:

> I think, brethren, we have been a little careless, and hereafter perhaps it would be wise for us to be more specific in our prayers. We have been praying to God for the conversion of sinners. But we have not told Him what kind of sinners we desired to save. He has saved, as we hope, this sinful woman and we don't know what to do—whether to receive her or not. Perhaps if we should be a little more careful hereafter to tell the Lord just what kind of sinners to convert, we may not have to be troubled.

His good humour won the day. His well-chosen words removed all opposition and the woman was unanimously voted into membership. She became one of the most dedicated and respected members of the church.

William clearly had a remarkable gift for reconciling opposing factions. He often brought harmony where there was discord. The Rev. George Hatt, a pastor at the Tabernacle, gave an excellent example of the gentle way William brought people together: 'In an eminent degree he was a peacemaker. If anything occurred to disturb the harmony of the body, he would rise with a pleasant smile and say, "Brethren, let us remember we are in His presence who taught us to love one another."'

In addition to great tact and diplomacy, William possessed tremendous warmth. It was this that so endeared him to people. Professor Harvey of the Hamilton theological school gives a revealing example:

My earliest recollection of Deacon Colgate is connected with the Baptist Tabernacle in Mulberry Street. I observed on entering that two men were acting as ushers. One was Deacon Colgate. I can never forget the warm, genial greeting received from him, nor probably would any stranger forget it. Dignity and kindness were so perfectly blended in the whole expression of the man, and the welcome was so thoroughly hearty that you were inevitably won and at once made at home. The stranger thus welcomed was quite sure to come again.

William's warmth also shone through in his lessons as a Bible class teacher. Years later many of his pupils recalled with affection how he put his points across with great clarity but it was the warm, relaxed manner in which he did so that made the deepest impression on them.

A new factory

Throughout his life William's church commitments always took priority over his business activities. He would decline social and business invitations if they clashed with enquiry meetings for individuals who wanted to know about the Christian faith and he rarely allowed business concerns to prevent him from attending prayer meetings. However, this had no effect on the growth of his company. It continued to develop at a phenomenal rate. Everyone wanted his soap.

The company remained very much a family concern. In 1838 his son Samuel joined the business as an apprentice at the age of sixteen. Six years later, in 1844, he was made a partner together with Bowles's son, Charles.

By 1847 demand for Colgate soap was so high that a more effective means of production became a matter of urgency. A soap-building kettle with a 43,000-pound capacity was felt to be the answer. A kettle of this size was unheard of in the industry at that time and the very idea met with ridicule in many quarters. Nevertheless construction went ahead and when finished it was such a curiosity that crowds were drawn to Dutch Street to see 'Colgate's Folly', as it had become known. But the scoffers were proved wrong. In the course of the next two years the kettle proved such a success that it too was unable to keep up with demand.

The only way to significantly increase production was to build a new factory, and the search began for a suitable site. As nowhere in New York City could be found that met the company's needs the net was cast wider to include locations across the Hudson River. An ideal site on the Jersey City waterfront was eventually discovered close to a convenient rail network and the Erie Canal. Building work started immediately. The new factory became the centre of production but Dutch Street remained the administrative base and also the location of the sales rooms.

Volunteer with the New York City Fire Department

By the time the new factory opened, William was one of the wealthiest men in New York City. He was also one of the city's most influential Christians. Despite the many pressures on his time from his business and church commitments, he somehow managed to find time to serve faithfully as treasurer for the New York City Fire Department in a wholly voluntary capacity for twenty-seven years.

Invitation to become Mayor of New York

However, he drew the line at involvement in politics. At a time when the administration of New York City was known to be corrupt to the core, he was invited to accept the nomination for Mayor. It was widely felt that he was the right man to restore the integrity of the mayoral office. His character, organizational abilities and leadership qualities were unquestioned and made him the ideal person to govern the city. Although he recognized it was a great honour to be considered for this prestigious position, he declined. Quite simply, his church and business commitments made it impossible for him to find enough time to do justice to the demands of the role.

The joy of home life

In the midst of his many responsibilities, William found great joy in the company of his family. He and Mary were loving parents to their nine children and their home was full of warmth, joy and laughter.

The large number of children ensured it would be a lively household with much fun and chatter but William never allowed conversations to sink to the level of idle gossip or unkind criticism. If he heard a negative comment about someone, he would immediately put a stop to it with a gentle rebuke, saying: 'If we can say nothing good of our neighbours, let us not say anything evil.'

He himself was a born conversationalist. Contemporaries acknowledged that his wide reading, keen observation of human behaviour and up-to-date knowledge of current affairs combined with good humour ensured he was always interesting to listen to.

William and Mary's Christian faith underpinned the loving atmosphere of their home. Daily prayer and Bible reading were a central feature of family life. Even at a time when cholera was rampant in New York City one summer and the family had to escape to rented rooms in a farmhouse in the country, their worship times continued as normal. Very early during their stay they invited all thirteen members of their host family to join them, an invitation that was accepted even though the family were not believers. The reality and sincerity of the Colgates' faith so touched their hosts that they continued to join in the worship times throughout the summer. Many years later a member of that family told one of William's sons that the worship times with the Colgates had been very precious and as a result all thirteen members of the family in turn became Christians.

The love, warmth and joy of the Colgate home was readily extended to visitors and it became renowned for its exceptional hospitality. So many pastors, evangelists and missionaries stayed there that it was often referred to as the 'Baptist Hotel'. Professor Harvey, who knew William well, recalls the healing effect the Colgate home had on him when he was suffering from depression:

> It was my privilege, while an invalid, to be a guest for several months in his family at the old John Street mansion, the delightful home so familiar and dear to many of our older missionaries and ministers, who were always welcomed there with such genial and large hospitality. The sunny atmosphere which pervaded the household seemed to diffuse itself from the head through all the members of it, and had the peculiar charm of putting the guest at once at his ease and making him at home. . . . To me, an invalid suffering from mental depression, his cheerful presence and the quickening atmosphere of that home were a perpetual tonic and inspiration. . . . that genuine Christian home lives before me as one of the sunniest and most blessed spots associated with my earlier life.

Dr Edward Lathrop, William and Mary's pastor at the Tabernacle Church for many years, also gives a glowing account of the Colgates' hospitality:

He was emphatically a kind-hearted man and a gentleman. His door was always open to the worthy stranger and to friends, especially to ministerial friends, when on visits of business or recreation to the city. His hearty manner, his cheerfulness, and above all his wealth of Christian sympathy, made him the centre of attraction to all, as well the young as the more aged, whose happiness it was to dwell under his roof. He was well mated also, for in his most estimable wife he found a companion who fully sympathized with him in the ministration of his generous hospitality, as she did indeed in all his benevolent schemes.

In 1845, after thirty-three years in their John Street home, the family moved to 128 Chambers Street and then, six years later, to 22 East 23rd Street, closer to the Tabernacle Church. Generous hospitality was a feature of every home they lived in and was an expression of their Christian love for others. But their love was also shown in other ways that very few would have been aware of. It was a purely private matter. If, for example, William discovered that a pastor, evangelist or missionary was in financial difficulty, he would quietly and unobtrusively press a cheque into his hand to ease his burden.

Facing death

Their home on East 23rd Street was to be their last. Their forty-four years of happily married life came to an end when Mary died there after failing health on 5 March 1855 aged sixty-six. Her death deeply affected William and his own health began to decline. During the course of the next two years he developed a crippling illness which gave him ever-increasing pain. An operation offered temporary relief but six weeks before his death the pain intensified, causing him to cry out: 'Oh, why must I suffer thus? I cannot tell—it is dreadful—but the Master knows; He knows and it is all right. It is to wean me from the world and prepare me for a better country.'

He patiently endured his sufferings and in the intervals when the pain was less severe he spent time reflecting on spiritual things. During one of these times of reflection he realized how blessed he was to have found a relationship with God long before pain and imminent death might have provided the motive to look for Him:

> How strange it is that any can delay the preparation for death till they come to the bed of pain! How ungrateful to God to let go the time of

health without answering His demands, and yield to Him nothing but sick-bed, broken thoughts! . . . Thanks to the Lord who led me to think of Him before my flesh failed me! What folly to put off repentance to a dying bed! For who knows what anguish may distract the mind and keep it from rising above its pains?

In his suffering he found that singing some of his favourite hymns was a great comfort and helped keep him in a positive frame of mind. A week before he died any lingering negativity there might have been had totally disappeared: 'Oh, I am so happy! I never felt so happy in my life. I love Jesus so.' His daughter Sarah, knowing the end was near, was clearly distressed but he tried to reassure her, saying, 'Do not mourn for me. Why should you? I shall be at rest. Think of it! An eternity with Christ!'

William died on Wednesday, 26 March 1857 aged seventy-four. He met the end joyfully. Raising his arms, his final words were, 'My precious Jesus!'

The Tabernacle Church was filled to overflowing for his funeral. The service was conducted by the pastor, Dr Edward Lathrop, whom William had faithfully served as a deacon for the past thirteen years. People of all classes and creeds were present, among them William's employees, many of whom were in tears. When the funeral was over, his coffin was transported to Greenwood Cemetery in Brooklyn where he was laid to rest with Mary.

Shortly before he died William had told his family: 'Trust in the Lord and remember how death brings you face to face with the life you live.' It was a reality check he had clearly applied to himself. Looking back he was no doubt grateful for the full and useful life he had lived and the many blessings he had received. And it was a life that can still inspire us today. We can admire the incredible success he achieved as a businessman, establishing a company that was to become one of the most famous in the world, without comprising his Christian faith. He convincingly showed that there need be no incompatibility between business practice and Christian values. Professor Harvey highlights this in a tribute to William:

> Rarely have I met one in whom religion had become so thoroughly incorporated, and, if I may so speak, naturalized as an ever-present power. While not slothful in business, and incessant in his devotion to it, he was also fervent in spirit, serving the Lord; and few men have so perfectly learned the secret of 'worship in work'. His business was

prosecuted as God's business, and it never seemed to require an effort on his part to turn from it and engage in prayer or religious conversation; but he appeared to be ever in the Spirit, living in the sight of spiritual realities.

The brand expands

On William's death in 1857, the presidency of the company passed to his son Samuel, thirty-five, and the business was renamed Colgate & Company. Samuel was in every way his father's son, seamlessly combining his business and religious interests. As well as head of an ever-expanding company he was a leading figure in many Christian organizations in the New York region. He was also President of the International YMCA.

Samuel, his wife Elizabeth and their seven children lived in Orange, New Jersey, where their home, like Samuel's childhood home, was full of love with the Bible and prayer at its heart. Samuel's Christian faith was equally as strong as his father's. It led him to help establish the North Orange Baptist Church which he served faithfully as trustee, deacon and Sunday school superintendent until his death. There is no better indication of his character than the comment of one child in the Sunday school to their teacher about the nature of God: 'I know what God is like. He is like Mr Colgate.'

Just as William was gifted with acute business acumen, so too was Samuel. Although the company was already flourishing, he saw scope for further expansion. Knowing that soap was regarded as nothing more than an object of practical use, he was convinced he could increase sales if he could enhance its appeal by giving it a pleasant smell. And so, in 1866, the Colgate company began the production of perfumed soap. It was an instant success. Soon afterwards he experimented with the manufacture of a range of perfumes. These too met with instant success.

Although the company's prosperity and reputation were initially built on soap, it is with toothpaste that its name is now most closely associated. This, again, was due to Samuel's vision. In 1873 he began the mass production of toothpaste in a jar and in 1896 introduced Colgate's Ribbon Dental Cream. That name means little to us today but it was a product that was to establish the Colgate brand worldwide—it was toothpaste in a tube. In fact, the words 'Colgate' and 'toothpaste' have now become virtually synonymous.

On 23 April 1897, just a year after introducing the company's most famous product, Samuel died. The day before his funeral, his brother James wrote a moving entry in his diary capturing Samuel's essential qualities: 'None but his family and nearest friends will know how good a man he was in all his relations to his family, kindred, church and country. His character is without blemish. His modesty and unobtrusiveness were proverbial. His steadfastness and tenacity to principle were remarkable. His devotion to Christ was the pivotal point of his power.'

Colgate University

William would have been delighted that the standards he had set and the foundations he had laid were built upon so admirably by Samuel. But his legacy lived on in other ways, too.

As we saw earlier, he was a member of the Board of Trustees of the Hamilton Literary and Theological Institution, a school originally intended for students training for the Christian ministry. When it later admitted students following a range of additional courses, it changed its name to Madison University. William was appointed a trustee of the university and together with members of his family provided the funding for more than half its property.

Years later, in recognition of the Colgate family's exceptional generosity, the governing body approved a proposed change of name to Colgate University. James, who had personally donated millions of dollars, was strongly opposed to the idea and insisted that no name change should occur during his lifetime. He argued that the family's support had been given purely from a desire to promote Christian education, not for personal glory. When it became clear that the governing body was determined to proceed with the change, James relented but only on condition that the name should be adopted in honour of his father William alone. On this understanding, Madison University became Colgate University in 1890. William's name thus lives on in the institution he loved so much and which is still thriving today.

William's legacy

His name and legacy were also given great prominence in the company's centenary year, 1906. Samuel's son Richard was now at the helm and under his leadership the business had continued to grow at an astonishing rate.

Chapter 1

By that year the company was producing 160 varieties of toilet soap, 625 varieties of perfume as well as countless other products.

At the celebratory banquet for the company's one thousand employees on 20 January at the Grand Central Palace, New York City, Richard made the following announcement which, not surprisingly, was most warmly received: 'We take pleasure in announcing that everyone now connected with Colgate and Company will receive a five-dollar gold piece for every completed year of continuous service.'

It would have given him great joy to make that announcement but without doubt it would have given him even greater joy—coupled with justifiable pride—that the company's past hundred years had seen no change in its ethos or values. His grandfather's legacy was still clearly evident to all:

> Things have changed greatly in 100 years. Our methods of doing business, our methods of manufacturing, our methods of doing this work and that work have all changed, and we all rejoice in the change; but there is one change which I am thankful to say has not been made, and that is the old-fashioned, honest business methods of doing business that William Colgate founded.
>
> We want to grow. We want to increase. We are all Americans—but we do not wish to grow or increase at the expense of honesty and uprightness and strict business principles. When our salesmen dispose of our goods, we wish them to tell the truth in regard to them, and not exaggerate. If a man is wrapping up a cake of soap at our factory we expect him, if he sees anything the matter with it, to throw it aside. If any one of the girls in the perfumery department is filling a bottle or putting on a label and that bottle is not full, is not as it should be, we expect it to be thrown aside. We wish to have honest goods.

The canal boat captain who had prayed for a despondent William Colgate on a towpath in Baltimore and lifted his spirits with God-given words of encouragement would have smiled to hear those words.

THOMAS COOK,
travel pioneer

There is no name in the world more immediately recognizable in connection with travel than Thomas Cook, the founder of a business empire which, at its peak, was worth billions. Yet the furthermost thought from Thomas Cook's mind when he organized his first ever railway excursion was making money. Throughout his career as a tour organizer his sense of service to others was paramount. His life's mission and greatest passion was to bring 'man nearer to man and nearer to his Creator' by making travel affordable and accessible to all.

Painful early years

Nothing in Thomas's early life remotely suggested it would lead to him becoming a household name across the globe. Born at 9 Quick Close, Melbourne, Derbyshire, on 22 November 1808, he was the son of a labourer, John Cook, who died in 1812, when Thomas was only three. Later that year his mother Elizabeth married James Smithard, also a labourer, and had two sons with him, James and Simeon.

The early years of his life in Melbourne were marked by considerable pain and hardship. Money was so tight in the household that Thomas had to leave school at the age of ten to supplement the family income. He was employed by John Roby, a market gardener and a heavy drinker. His first job assisting Roby was in the gardens of Melbourne Hall. The work was physically demanding. It involved fetching and carrying heavy sacks and baskets and a considerable amount of digging.

Roby's addiction to alcohol put extra strain on Thomas. Roby was often the worse for wear after a drinking bout and incapable of selling the estate's garden produce in the neighbouring villages. It was left to Thomas to take on this extra work.

In 1820 Thomas had an even greater burden to bear when his kind and supportive stepfather, James Smithard, died. It was the second time in his childhood that he had lost a father. Immediately after Smithard's burial, he was told by his mother: 'Now, Tommy, you must be father to these two boys.' A very heavy responsibility indeed for a twelve-year-old.

Sadly, his struggles seemed never-ending. Two years later he began a five-year apprenticeship as a wood-turner and cabinet-maker with his uncle, John Pegg. But Pegg, like Roby, was an alcoholic and once again Thomas found himself burdened with an increased workload because of drink. He later recalled: 'The turner sought his relaxation and enjoyment night after night in a snug corner in the village public house, where much of his time was wasted and his means so dissipated that, notwithstanding a good business, he lived and died a poor man.'

Witnessing the damaging effects of drink at close quarters over long periods scarred Thomas but, as we shall see, these disturbing experiences were to prove blessings in disguise. They led to his active involvement in the Temperance Movement, the fight against drink and the misery it caused, and this, in turn, became the springboard for his amazing career in the travel business.

'The earnest, active, devoted, young Christian'

It was during those years of struggle in his adolescence that the seeds of Thomas's deep Christian faith were sown. At the age of fourteen he began to attend the Sunday school of Melbourne Baptist Chapel at about the same time as the new minister, Joseph Winks, arrived. Winks had a profound guiding influence on him and Thomas looked up to him as a father. In the words of his good friend the Baptist pastor J. R. Godfrey, it was through Winks's ministry that his 'soul was won for Christ'. At the age of seventeen he felt ready to be baptized as a public confession of his faith.

Thomas showed such commitment in the Sunday school that he was promoted first to teacher, then to superintendent. He was described in the *General Baptist Magazine* as an 'earnest, active, devoted young Christian'.

During his time in Melbourne Winks launched the *Baptist Children's Magazine* and set up a printing press in Loughborough. He tried to combine his publishing activities with his ministry in Melbourne but found it impossible. He therefore left Melbourne in 1826 to devote himself to publishing magazines 'for the young and the poor'.

When Pegg's drinking became too much for Thomas he gave up his apprenticeship aged eighteen to join Winks in Loughborough to learn the art of printing and publishing.

The call to evangelism

While in Loughborough, Thomas became increasingly aware of the call to preach the gospel, the good news of God's gift of eternal life through Jesus Christ, His Son. And so, aged nineteen, with the full backing of Melbourne Baptist Chapel, he successfully applied to the General Baptist Missionary Society to become an evangelist. He was entrusted with the duties of 'village missionary, tract distributor, and Sunday school promoter' to serve in a number of localities in the Midlands.

Although it gave him great joy to preach in country chapels and on village greens, the work of an itinerant evangelist was demanding. It required wholehearted devotion, unfailing energy and unflagging perseverance in the face of fierce opposition. There was no financial incentive to accept the calling. Thomas's income was meagre and, as he couldn't afford stagecoach travel, he had to walk incredibly long distances. In 1829 alone he covered more than two thousand miles on foot.

He also met with ridicule and contempt. Despite his kindly manner and warm smile, his preaching style was forceful and direct and he pulled no punches in confronting immorality. As a result, stones and other objects were thrown at him and he was physically assaulted. But he took all this in his stride. His fearlessness and passion for his work made him more than a match for the hecklers whose hissing he laughingly dismissed as 'Gooseism and Snakeism'.

Marriage

Thomas served as an evangelist for three years but then the funds of the Baptist Missionary Society ran out. As he needed to make a living, he set up in business as a wood-turner in the village of Barrowden in Rutland. He was drawn there because of his affection for Marianne Mason, a farmer's daughter he had met two years previously at the Baptist chapel in Barrowden while an evangelist. Marianne was a teacher at the Sunday school. She kept house for her widower father and looked after her five younger brothers. Thomas lodged with the family while he worked in the village.

However, there proved to be too little work for a wood-turner in

Barrowden and so, in November 1832, Thomas relocated to Market Harborough with its larger population. He rented a house in Adam and Eve Street and very quickly earned enough to provide for a wife and family. He therefore proposed to Marianne and on 2 March 1833 they were married at St Peter's Church in Barrowden. Thomas was twenty-four, Marianne twenty-six. Adam and Eve Street became their home for the next eight and a half years. Their first child, John Mason Cook, was born there in January 1834.

The energetic anti-drink campaigner

The move to Market Harborough on his own before his marriage had opened an important new chapter in Thomas's life. It was here that he became actively involved in the Temperance Movement, the crusade against drink, one of the biggest social problems of his day.

Pubs and so-called gin palaces offered a cheap and easily available form of escape from the mind-numbing conditions in which most workers lived. Their working hours were long and hard, their income was pitifully low and there were few, if any, home comforts. Families in towns lived in cramped, squalid conditions and there was little to cheer the spirit. To make matters worse, money that should have been spent on food and clothing was often squandered on drink. Alcohol-fuelled behaviour also became a problem in the streets where the sight of drunken brawls was all too common.

Not surprisingly, alcohol became the target of well-meaning social reformers. In 1832 Joseph Livesey founded the Preston Temperance Society which marked the birth of the Temperance Movement in England. The movement soon became associated in the public mind with the term 'teetotalism'. It was famously coined by one of Joseph Livesey's supporters, Richard Turner, a reformed alcoholic, when he defiantly stuttered: 'I'll have nowt to do with the moderation botheration pledge; I'll be reet down t-t-total, that or nowt.'

Temperance campaigners formed national, regional and local societies open to any adult who signed a pledge to abstain from alcohol. They worked tirelessly to educate the public about the dangers of drink and created alcohol-free recreational facilities such as coffee houses, reading rooms, libraries, museums and parks as an alternative to pubs and gin palaces. They also arranged wholesome entertainment including concerts, singing, drama, readings and recitations.

Thomas's involvement with temperance began when he joined the Market Harborough Baptist Church of which the Rev. Francis Beardsall, an agent of the British and Foreign Temperance Society, was minister. Beardsall's preaching against the dangers of drink struck a chord with Thomas. He was only too well aware of these, having worked for two alcoholic employers. On New Year's Day 1833 he responded to Rev. Beardsall's appeal to sign the pledge agreeing 'to abstain from ardent spirits, and to discountenance the causes and practice of intemperance'.

The pledge at this stage applied only to spirits and Thomas, in fact, still kept beer and wine in his home. However, this changed in early December 1836 when he heard a teetotal lecture in Market Harborough town hall. It made such an impact on him that the next day he and six others formed the South Midland Temperance Association in the town. Thomas was appointed its secretary and from this time on he abstained from all forms of alcohol.

His commitment to the temperance cause was total. Fully supported by Marianne, he worked tirelessly as Secretary of the South Midland Temperance Association arranging meetings, attending conferences and organizing bazaars, galas and other events. He also became a renowned public speaker. During his time as an evangelist he had developed considerable skill as a preacher and his ability to hold an audience without the use of notes once more came into its own.

Thomas also drew on another important experience from his past: printing and publishing. He threw himself wholeheartedly—entirely at his own expense—into producing a whole range of materials supporting the message of abstinence. It was a measure of his commitment that the sales of his publications barely covered costs. Furthermore, time spent printing was lost from wood-turning and so, inevitably, money was always tight.

Violent opposition

As Thomas had discovered in his time as an evangelist, not everyone wanted to hear his message. Once again he met with violent opposition, this time from brewers, publicans and their supporters. Fuelled by hatred they hired thugs to attack temperance workers in the streets and damage their homes. Meetings in the Market Harborough town hall were almost always broken up. Thomas was booed, hissed and sneered at in the streets and stones were thrown at him. He vividly recalled the time: 'My house in Adam and Eve Street was violently assailed, and brick bats came flying through the window to the imminent danger of Mrs Cook and myself. On one occasion a horse's leg bone taken from a cartload of bones was thrown at me with such violence that, striking me at the back of the neck, I was felled to the ground.' However, he was able to chase and catch his attacker and have him brought to court to face a hefty fine.

Far from weakening his resolve to fight against alcohol, ugly opposition merely served to strengthen it. It made him more determined than ever to find alternative forms of recreation to drink. Quite unexpectedly, on 9 June 1841, he hit on an idea that was to have far-reaching consequences . . .

A ground-breaking idea

That day he set out from Market Harborough on a fifteen-mile walk to Leicester to attend a quarterly meeting of temperance delegates. As he was passing the Congregational Chapel in Kibworth Harcourt, the recent extension of the railway network suddenly came into his mind and in a flash of inspiration he realized its possibilities. He recalled the moment many years later:

> From my residence at Market Harborough I walked to Leicester (fifteen miles) to attend that meeting. About midway between Harborough and Leicester—my mind's eye has often reverted to that spot—a thought flashed through my brain—what a glorious thing it would be if the newly developed powers of railways and locomotion could be made subservient to the promotion of temperance!

By the time he had reached the venue, the idea was fully formed in his mind. Addressing the delegates, he proposed that their next quarterly meeting in Loughborough should be turned into a special event on a non-profit basis. His plan was to charter a train as cheaply as possible from Leicester to Loughborough and back and arrange a fun day out for the public in a carnival atmosphere but with a series of temperance messages at the end. The response to his idea could not have been better: 'The Chairman approved, the meeting roared with excitement, and early next day I proposed my grand scheme to John Fox Bell, the resident secretary of the Midland Counties Railway Company.'

Bell was also fully supportive. He not only gave his approval but also made a donation towards the cost of the event.

Cook's first railway excursion

Thomas immediately began planning the excursion. He secured cheap railway fares and made arrangements with a keen temperance supporter, William Paget, to hold a gala in his private park in Loughborough. He then advertised the event.

His hard work paid off. On Monday, 5 July 1841, some five hundred passengers assembled at Leicester's Campbell Street Station to embark on their ten-mile journey. It was believed to be the largest number to travel on a train. Such was the novelty of the occasion that over two thousand people turned up at the station to witness their departure. A brass band added to the colour of the occasion.

Despite all the excitement some of the passengers were nervous of travelling by rail for the first time. And with good reason. Nine of the ten carriages had no seats and no roofs and they accommodated as many people as could be squeezed in. There was no protection from rain, smoke, soot or sparks.

Thomas felt it essential, therefore, to escort the party personally to give them reassurance. He was always concerned for the comfort, safety and well-being of his clients and wanted to share with them not only the pleasures of travel but also the difficulties and hardships. This became a feature of all his pioneering excursions.

There was huge public interest in the event. Thomas wrote: 'People crowded the streets, filled windows, covered the house-tops, and cheered us all along the line with the heartiest welcome.' The *Leicester Chronicle* reported that 'every bridge along the line was crowded to have a peep at the train in progress'.

The train's arrival at Loughborough Station met with unbelievable excitement from some two thousand people who had gathered to welcome the excursionists. The carnival atmosphere began immediately as the intrepid passengers were led by a brass band from the station to William

Paget's park. There they were joined by local people and others who had travelled from nearby Midlands towns.

In total some three thousand people participated in the gala. They presented a colourful spectacle with many carrying flags and banners and decked out in temperance rosettes, ribbons and medals. The afternoon was spent in a whole range of leisure activities including cricket, dancing and games such as blind man's bluff and tag. It was a measure of Thomas's organizational skills that he provided a substantial picnic for all three thousand participants at teatime.

The serious part of the day began at 6 p.m. For the next three hours the crowd listened to a series of rousing speeches by church ministers warning them of the dangers of drink. Today this would seem a most unusual way of rounding off a day of fun and frivolity but at the time gifted public speakers who could hold an audience spellbound were often seen as an exciting form of entertainment.

When the event drew to a close, Thomas's party made their way back to Loughborough Station for the return journey to Leicester. On arrival in Leicester at 10.30 p.m. they were enthusiastically welcomed by a huge crowd impressed by their pioneering spirit. The expedition had clearly been a massive success. As Thomas wrote, 'the whole affair . . . excited extraordinary interest, not only in the county of Leicester but throughout the whole country'.

It is difficult for us to understand today why this ten-mile railway excursion should create so much excitement and become the focus of national interest. Perhaps if we imagine the likely reaction when the first large-scale tourist trip into outer space takes place, we might get some idea of how Thomas's achievement appeared in the eyes of his contemporaries. He himself recognized the significance of the event and always looked back on it as the birth of his career in the travel business.

Struggling printing business in Leicester

The success of the Loughborough excursion fired Thomas's imagination and inspired him to want to organize more in the cause of temperance. He felt it would make sound practical sense to move to Leicester with its good rail connections in pursuit of this aim. He also saw the possibility of earning a better living there by setting up in business as a printer and publisher. And so, two months after the Loughborough trip, Thomas set up his new home and printing business at 1 King Street producing temperance literature and Baptist devotional works.

But his energies were not limited to printing and publishing. In 1843 he opened a temperance hotel (run by Marianne) at 28 Granby Street, Leicester, which served as the family home and his business HQ. He also continued his tireless work as Secretary of the South Midland Temperance Association.

However, despite vigorously promoting his products, his business struggled, not least because he continually subsidized his unprofitable temperance publications. Although he ran a number of sidelines such as book-binding and the sale of stationery and pens, they did not cover his costs. In July 1843 he wrote that he had 'suffered great pecuniary losses and disappointments in his endeavours to serve the cause of true temperance'.

Alongside his business activities, Thomas organized several cheap excursions to temperance events for 'rational and exquisite enjoyment'. But they brought no income, being run as a labour of love on a non-profit basis. As he later explained: 'The work was one of enthusiastic philanthropy bringing with it its own reward, for during that time I never dreamt of it as a source of pecuniary interest.'

By 1844, no doubt because of his financial pressures and the birth of a baby due in June the following year (his daughter Annie), he began to turn his thoughts to the potential of commercial tourism as an additional source of income. Aware that he had established a reputation as an outstanding travel organizer, he clearly felt this was a realistic step to take. Providentially, his financial pressures were to prove a gateway to an exciting new direction in his career.

First commercial excursion: Liverpool and North Wales

Thomas's first step was to select a destination for his first commercial excursion. He decided on a trip from Leicester to Liverpool, an attractive city with many grand buildings and the gateway to the New World. From Liverpool his party would proceed by steamer to North Wales to visit Caernarfon and its magnificent castle and then ascend the mountain path to the summit of Snowdon.

Thomas soon discovered that planning the journey was not

straightforward. The train from Leicester to Liverpool ran on the lines of three different railway companies, each issuing their own separate tickets, and his first task was to try to convince these companies to issue a single ticket valid across their lines. He successfully negotiated an agreement with them then tried out the route himself. When everything was in place, he produced *The Handbook of the Trip to Liverpool* with the full itinerary and information about the sights to be visited.

With everything in place he set about advertising the trip. As the price was low the response was unbelievable. The 1,200 available tickets were quickly snapped up and such was the demand that many were re-sold at exorbitant prices.

Thomas's first commercial tourist excursion departed Leicester at 5 a.m. on Monday, 4 August 1845 with himself in accompaniment. After a short stay in Liverpool, 350 of the party continued by steamer to Caernarfon. Their arrival there caused a sensation. It was the largest group of tourists ever seen in this Welsh-speaking town. Fortunately someone was found who spoke enough English to act as their guide. After the tour and a visit to the castle, the next objective was Snowdon, Thomas leading the party up the footpath to the summit.

Such was the success of the excursion that the *Leicester Chronicle* enthused: 'a more agreeable, rational and delightful amusement it is difficult to conceive'. A fortnight later Thomas repeated it with a group of 800 and it was another huge success. Overjoyed by the winning formula he had discovered, he quickly saw its potential for further development and wrote in his diary: 'From the heights of Snowdon my thoughts took flight to Ben Lomond, and I determined to try to get to Scotland.' He clearly had the beautiful scenery of Loch Lomond in his mind and the appeal for tourists of sailing on its waters.

A dream realized

With Scotland now firmly in his sights, Thomas made two exploratory visits there to find the most practical route. This was essential as there was no rail link from England. He finally decided the best way would be by rail from Leicester to Fleetwood, from there by steamer to Ardrossan and then on to Glasgow and Edinburgh by rail. Edinburgh would serve as the base for excursions to locations of scenic or historic interest.

To keep the price as low as possible he had to convince the rail and steamship companies that it would be more profitable for them to transport large numbers of passengers at a reduced fare than a small number at the normal rate. He managed to agree terms with them and then compiled a *Handbook of a Trip to Scotland* with information for the excursionists. With everything in place he duly advertised the trip and on 25 June 1846 his party of 350 set off from Leicester Station.

At first, through no fault of Thomas's, everything went wrong. Stops had been arranged en route to Fleetwood for refreshments and the use of toilet facilities (there were none on trains at the time) but they didn't happen. The situation was made worse when it was discovered there were too few cabins on the steamer for everyone and many passengers, including Thomas, had to spend the rain-lashed, windswept night on deck. There was to be a serious backlash from these setbacks.

Nevertheless, the rest of the trip exceeded all expectations. When the train pulled into Glasgow's Bridge Street Station guns were fired in salute. It was the biggest tourist party the city had ever seen and they were led by a brass band to a reception in the city hall.

The next stop was Edinburgh. As in Glasgow, the party's arrival met with great excitement. Once again they were welcomed at the station by a band which then escorted them through the streets. In the excursionists' honour a special musical event had been arranged for them in the evening by the renowned publisher and temperance advocate William Chambers.

From Edinburgh the tour continued to locations of particular interest, one of which was Loch Lomond. The party enjoyed sailing on this beautiful lake in the midst of stunning scenery. How satisfying this must have been for Thomas! His vision on the summit of Snowdon had now been realized.

Financial collapse

But then he was landed a devastating blow. Despite the overwhelming success of the greater part of the trip, some of his party were still furious because of the inconveniences they had suffered on the outward journey. They decided to take legal action against him.

Thomas had already incurred heavy losses in subsidizing his temperance publications and now the costs of these lawsuits aggravated his already fragile financial position. He fell heavily into debt. As a result, an indenture issued on 31 July 1846 'assigned and transferred all his personal estate and effects' to his creditors. In August 1846 his household furniture was put up for sale and early in 1847 bankruptcy hearings were held in Nottingham. It was an extremely painful period for him but somehow, in a very short space of time, he managed to come to an agreement with his creditors and narrowly avoided the shame of bankruptcy.

Pressing on

Undeterred by this disturbing experience, Thomas pressed on with plans for further visits to Scotland. In the autumn of 1847—in an astute marketing move—he organized a tour following a route Queen Victoria and Prince Albert had recently taken to the Highlands and the Hebridean islands of Iona and Staffa. On stretches in remote areas where there were no railway lines, he arranged transport with horse-drawn coaches. Interestingly, the term 'sightseeing' was coined at this time.

When the party arrived on Iona, Thomas was dismayed to see the extreme poverty of the inhabitants. He wrote that it was 'impossible for tourists visiting the Hebridean district to be indifferent to, or unmoved by, the symptoms of destitution and distress'. He was determined to help the islanders. He managed to raise enough money to buy twenty-four boats fully equipped with nets and tackle to enable them to make a living from fishing. In gratitude to Thomas, the islanders named one of the boats after him. It gave him great joy to have been able to help them and he stated: 'There is a pleasure in these pursuits which selfishness can never appreciate.'

Sidelined by the railway companies

Just when it seemed that Thomas's tourist business was beginning to take off, the railway companies pulled the plug on him. The reason, quite simply, was that they felt they could run excursions themselves and make a bigger profit by cutting him out as the middleman. It looked as if he was heading for another financial disaster. But ever resourceful, if one avenue was closed to him he looked for another. With rail travel no longer available to him, he concentrated on visits to places of interest within striking distance of Leicester using horse-drawn coaches.

In August 1848 he organized the first of these local trips. It was to the gardens of Melbourne Hall where he had himself once worked. Although Lord Melbourne would not allow the Hall to be opened, the gardens themselves were attraction enough. Most of Melbourne's two thousand inhabitants turned out to witness the unusual spectacle of a brass band accompanying a procession of coaches carrying over a hundred visitors through their village.

This excursion was followed by a visit to Belvoir Castle, home of the Duke of Rutland. Lord Rutland recognized that Thomas was trying to break down the barriers between different classes by making travel affordable to all and he wrote to him: 'I fully concur with you in the desire which you express to see the different classes of our great community bound together by ties of increasing strength.' Six horse-drawn coaches took the excursionists to Belvoir Castle and such was the excitement that music was played at each village they passed through along the twenty-eight-mile route from Leicester.

The next stately residence to open its doors was Chatsworth House, the grand home of the Duke of Devonshire. The party was given a warm welcome by the Duke himself and to add to their enjoyment he proudly displayed his various collections.

The booming Scottish market

Thomas had found a ready market for his coach trips to local places of interest but in an unexpected change of heart the railway companies asked him to resume his services for them. They had found they just couldn't manage without him.

With the railways once again at his disposal, Thomas escorted two parties to Scotland in 1849 totalling about one thousand people. He also organized tours to North Wales, Ireland, the Isle of Man and Blackpool. By 1850 he had escorted over fifteen thousand passengers some 7,500 miles and was able to add 'Excursion Agent' to his advertised list of business activities.

He saw the Scottish market as the key to the phenomenal growth of his business and wrote that Scotland, 'almost imperceptibly, transformed me from a cheap excursion conductor to a tourist organizer and manager'. For all but one year between 1848 and 1863 he organized four annual excursions there, taking as many as five thousand people each season.

Grateful clients

Thomas was aware that many of his tourists were anxious about the journeys they faced and he took great pains to attend to them personally. In 1850, in recognition of his outstanding service, eight hundred grateful clients organized a 'Grand Testimonial Trip' to Cambridge to honour him at a specially arranged concert. During the interval he was presented with an inscribed gold watch and chain for 'having for nine years zealously and satisfactorily served the public' and for the 'opportunities of enjoyment' he had given.

Fired with enthusiasm he now turned his mind to wider horizons: 'By the end of the season of 1850 I had become so thoroughly imbued with the tourist spirit that I began to contemplate foreign trips, including the Continent of Europe, the United States, and the Eastern Lands of the Bible.'

The Crystal Palace and a national reputation

Intending to make America his first foreign destination, Thomas set off for Liverpool to explore the possibilities of transatlantic tourist travel. On the way he changed trains in Derby and happened to meet John Ellis, Chairman of the Midland Railway, and Joseph Paxton, a director of the railway and also the head gardener at Chatsworth. Thomas knew Ellis from excursion arrangements he had made with him in the past and he had met Paxton at Chatsworth House when he organized trips there.

They told him that Queen Victoria's husband, Prince Albert, was organizing the world's first international trade fair in Hyde Park, London, to give Britain and the rest of the world the opportunity to showcase their manufacturing achievements in a spirit of peace and friendship. Paxton had been commissioned to design the biggest glass structure in the world to house the exhibits. He had already established a reputation for building a greenhouse at Chatsworth—the Great Conservatory—which at the time was the world's largest glass building.

Thomas applauded Prince Albert's idea and the spirit behind it. As a central aim of all his excursions was to bring 'man nearer to man' he promptly agreed to Ellis and Paxton's request to suspend his American plans and organize rail excursions from the Midlands and the North to the fair instead. He stated passionately: 'If ever there was a time when the great power and astonishing facilities of Railways should be most fully exerted on behalf of the population generally, surely 1851 is that time.'

To ensure that low-paid manual workers should be able to visit the exhibition 'not as to a show or place of amusement but a great School of Science, of Art, of Industry, of Peace and Universal Brotherhood!' Thomas arranged cheap fares for them, even though it meant a big reduction in his own profits.

The Great Exhibition, as the fair was called, was opened by Queen Victoria on 1 May 1851. Paxton's impressive glass structure became known as 'the Crystal Palace' and attracted six million visitors—about a third of the population of Britain at the time—during the exhibition months May to October.

The Crystal Palace was designed rather like a Christian cathedral with nave, aisles and transepts. The nave was 1,848 feet (563 metres) long and its width was almost double that of St Paul's Cathedral. Internally it consisted of three levels of wrought iron galleries bearing the weight of thousands of tons of machinery. In total, 112,000 exhibits were displayed by Britain, forty-two British colonies and thirty-nine foreign countries.

With the help of his son John, now seventeen, Thomas transported 150,000 excursionists to London and back during the exhibition months. Travel was mostly through the night but some excursionists were not keen to spend the night on the train so Thomas arranged accommodation for them in London. But there was no such luxury for himself. He rarely spent a night at home, sleeping instead on the floor of the trains.

The Great Exhibition was a significant landmark in Thomas's career in the travel business. His careful planning and organization ensured that the trips ran very smoothly and earned him national recognition as an excursion organizer.

First tour abroad

Following the success of the Crystal Palace trips, Thomas led expeditions to other major exhibitions. He also organized circular tours in Ireland and Scotland. With the income he earned from these ventures he built new premises in 1853 at 123 Granby Street, Leicester, which served as a temperance hotel, his home and his business HQ. He also set up a soup kitchen for the poor there. Next door he built a temperance hall providing wholesome entertainment such as concerts, sketches and readings.

By 1854 his tourist work had become so time-consuming that he decided to devote himself wholly to it and give up his printing business. He was now forty-five.

A year later he felt ready to cross the English Channel for the first time and escorted a party of forty to Brussels and Paris, continuing with twenty-five of them on a Rhine cruise from Cologne to Strasbourg. He repeated this a month later with a group of fifty. Although neither tour was a commercial success, they met with the warm approval of the participants. After the first tour Thomas was presented with a testimonial of thanks by the party and given permission to quote their praise in his company magazine. His 'Christian manner' had deeply impressed them. He had left no stone unturned in his care for them and in his meticulous attention to detail in making the tour so enjoyable.

The tour also inspired a deep appreciation of the beauties of nature. One young woman wrote in her diary: 'the glorious sights that have filled my mind with such ideas of natural beauty, have also in some degree, purified and refined my thoughts and given me higher concepts of the Creator'. This was precisely the effect Thomas had hoped for. He stated that one of his main aims in taking parties abroad was to give as many as possible the opportunity 'to behold the handiwork of the Great Supreme' and thus bring people closer to God.

Another setback overcome: the glories of Switzerland

Despite the positive response of the tourists, Thomas suspended his trips abroad for a few years and concentrated on his Scottish tours. By 1860 some fifty thousand people had travelled with him there but two years later this door suddenly closed. Remarkably, as had happened before, the Scottish railway companies decided to replace him with their own personnel to increase their profits. It was a calamitous blow. Without Scotland Thomas's business could not survive. The future looked bleak. 'Beyond the present season all is in obscurity,' he wrote. But his trust in God was unshaken and he continued 'to follow the leadings of Providence'. It was to Switzerland he felt he was being directed: 'There are feelings which prompt the mind to the wide grasp of objects and labours across the English Channel, and fix, as it were, the standard of hope on the mountains of Switzerland.'

With Switzerland now in his sights, Thomas organized a preliminary tour to test the effectiveness of a circular railway ticket valid for one month starting and finishing in Paris on the Geneva, Lausanne and Neuchâtel route. On 26 June 1863 more than 130 tourists set off with him to Paris, sixty-two of whom continued with him to Geneva. From there the tourists were free to break into smaller groups to explore destinations of their own choosing. Thomas himself accompanied two small groups to Chamonix and Martigny at the heart of breathtaking Alpine scenery.

The circular ticket was a great success and Thomas organized two further trips to Switzerland that year. Writing from Paris on 4 August 1863, he could not hide his enthusiasm:

> France and Switzerland now present to me new and almost unlimited fields of tourist labour. At this moment I am surrounded in Paris with some 500 or 600 enterprising tourists, and am expecting an addition of 400 or 500 more tonight. Already a party of 100 has started for Switzerland and I expect to follow them tomorrow with 260 to 300 more. . . . This is, I believe, the largest party that ever left England for a tour of Switzerland.

In the summer of 1864, in another dramatic about-turn, the Scottish railway companies realized they couldn't manage without Thomas's expertise and invited him to return to their fold. But this time he declined. He had successfully replaced his Scottish business with Continental tours and these fully occupied him. In fact, they were so popular that he began to cast his net ever wider. On 4 July 1864 he set off on his first tour of Italy visiting Rome, Naples, Pompeii and Mount Vesuvius with a party of over ninety. The success of this tour resulted in a very quick repeat. Providentially, the closing of the Scottish door had opened an even wider one in continental Europe.

'God's earth is for the people'

Thomas was enjoying huge success but profit was never his main motive. He had much higher ideals. When outlining his plans for one of his Italian trips, he made it clear that 'any who cannot accompany us in a genial, sociable and confiding spirit will be kind enough not to join our parties. . . . We have been accustomed to look upon our work in the character of a mission of goodwill and universal brotherhood.' He was convinced that foreign travel could break down distrust between nations and believed that if people of different nationalities actually met each other they would discover that they shared a common humanity. This, he argued, would encourage peace and help remove the constant threat of war.

Thomas always insisted that his excursions fostered 'enlargement to mind and deepening of charity' and wrote: 'It is delightful to see, as we travel on, the breaking down of partition walls of prejudice . . . the expansion of the intellect . . . the benevolent sympathies excited by a more extended knowledge of the circumstances and sufferings of fellow creatures'. He also observed that 'Christian ministers of various creeds and churches have thrown off the asperities of sectarianism and have sung, prayed and fraternized together in many exercises of devotion, praise and charity'.

But his noble aims triggered fierce opposition. Not for the first time he became the target of ridicule and contempt. He offended people who believed that he was encouraging the wrong type of person to travel to locations that should remain the exclusive preserve of the upper classes. His tourists were scathingly dismissed as 'low-bred', 'stupid', 'a mob', 'Cook's Circus' and 'Cook's Hordes'. How could they possibly appreciate the wonders of nature or the glories of art and architecture?

Despite the fact that his tourists were impeccably well behaved and appreciative of all that they saw, prejudice against them persisted. Thomas was infuriated by the arrogant attitude of snobs who wanted to 'reserve statue and mountain, painting and lake, historical association and natural beauty for the so-called upper classes'. He made his position perfectly clear to them: 'I see no sin in introducing natural and artistic wonders to all'; and he stressed that 'God's earth with all its fullness and beauty is for the people'.

To America

But no amount of criticism could hold him back. Having opened up Europe he decided to visit America to explore its potential as a tourist destination, a realistic possibility with the ending of the American Civil War in 1865. Furthermore, he now had sufficient time as he had confidently entrusted his son John with the full-time administration of the business at the company's new headquarters in London which had opened that year in Fleet Street. John was a dynamic character who, in addition to his administrative responsibilities, travelled some fifty thousand miles annually consolidating existing markets and opening up new ones. In recognition of his substantial contribution to the business he was eventually made a full partner in 1872 when the company's name was changed to Thomas Cook and Son.

Thomas set off for America on 29 November 1865 sailing from Liverpool to New York. From there he started an exploratory tour of both the USA and Canada to gauge their market potential. He spent eleven weeks away travelling some four thousand miles by rail. His journey took in Philadelphia, 'the great Quaker city', where he spent a 'marvellously quiet' Sunday; Washington DC; Springfield, Illinois, where he visited the home and tomb of Abraham Lincoln who had been assassinated a few months earlier; Chicago; the spectacular Niagara Falls; and Montreal. It was an indication of his priorities that he wrote home to Marianne to tell her about the deep impression a service at a Baptist chapel in New York City had made on him.

In the spring of 1866, just two months after Thomas's return, John led a tour following his father's trail. Although no further tours took place on that continent for seven years, John eventually established America as a popular tourist destination. One of his great achievements was the launch of his 'Circular Notes' there in 1874. These were the forerunners of travellers' cheques which saved tourists carrying large amounts of money with them. It was a similar idea to the hotel coupons the company had introduced six years previously which were exchangeable for accommodation and meals. The Circular Notes were a runaway success and in 1878 Cook's Banking and Exchange Department was opened to cater for the demand.

The Holy Land: 'The greatest event of my tourist life'

As a devout Christian Thomas had long felt drawn to the Holy Land 'to trace out sites and scenes immortalized in the Bible'. At the end of 1868 he made an exploratory trip to Egypt and Palestine (modern-day Israel) to assess their viability as tourist destinations.

It was a courageous step. He had been warned there were no railways or proper roads in Palestine and that coach travel there was impossible. There was also the ever-present threat of robbery. In fact, those who knew that region advised travellers to go armed and with an escort. This would be no trip for the faint-hearted.

Undeterred by these drawbacks, Thomas assembled an intrepid party of thirty-two who left London on 24 January 1869 for a 105-day tour of

Egypt and the Holy Land. After crossing the Mediterranean from Brindisi to Alexandria, the party continued their journey by rail to Cairo where two steamers were hired to take them up the Nile to Giza to visit the Pyramids and the Sphinx and then to Luxor to explore the Valley of the Kings. After a truly memorable stay in Egypt, the party set off for Palestine and the gruelling part of their tour.

After the sea crossing from Alexandria to Beirut, the hardy tourists endured up to eight hours a day on horseback, spending the nights in tents. They made their way through difficult, hot, dusty terrain to some of the most familiar-sounding locations in the Bible—Bethlehem, Jericho, the River Jordan, the Dead Sea and, of course, Jerusalem.

As expected, not everything went well. While camping outside the walls of Jerusalem the party was robbed and a considerable amount of money stolen. However, the culprits were quickly apprehended and compelled to repay the stolen money. In addition, one of the thieves was ordered by the authorities to hand over a house he owned in Bethlehem to Thomas, who unhesitatingly donated it to the Society for the Promotion of Christianity Among the Jews, one of the many missions he supported.

The Middle Eastern tour, despite its difficulties and discomforts, made a deep impression on the party. They were well aware that Thomas had smoothed their path as much as humanly possible and in gratitude to him for his care and attention they signed a testimonial in recognition of the 'honourable, efficient and straightforward manner in which he has fulfilled his engagements'.

For Thomas, this was much more than a trip to a distant country—it was a pilgrimage. He afterwards told the *Leicester Journal* that it was 'the greatest event of my tourist life'.

Enthused by the success of the tour, Thomas organized more, ever conscious of their spiritual benefits. Looking back after four years of leading visits to the Holy Land, he wrote with considerable pleasure: 'the educational and social results of these four years of Eastern travel have been most encouraging. A new incentive to scriptural investigation has been created and fostered.' He went on to establish 'Biblical, Educational and General Tours for Ministers, Sunday school teachers and others engaged in promoting scriptural education'.

By 1891, the company's fiftieth anniversary, some twelve thousand pilgrims had used his services to travel to the Middle East. Among them were leading members of European royalty, including the future King of England, George V. The mockers who had disparaged Cook's tourists as 'low-bred' and 'a mob' had to eat their words.

First round-the-world tour

Thomas's next great challenge was to circle the globe. He had attended the opening ceremony of the Suez Canal on 16 November 1869, the 102-mile canal which made it possible for ships to travel between Europe and India by connecting the Mediterranean Sea and the Red Sea. The previous route had been around Africa, 4,300 miles longer. The canal also reduced the voyage time from England to Australia from eight weeks to five.

This phenomenal work of engineering opened up new and exciting possibilities for Thomas. He wrote early in 1870:

> Thirty years have passed since the first thought of applying the powers
> and facilities of railways and locomotion to the purpose of social and
> benevolent organization led to proposals and labours which have
> culminated in visits to Jerusalem, to the land of Pharaohs, to Asia and
> Greece: and now we are pressed to go wider still, to Circumnavigate the
> World.

On 26 September 1872, now sixty-three, he set off from Liverpool for New York with nine companions on the first ever leisure trip around the globe. It was a 25,000-mile journey that would take 222 days. The party travelled from New York across the USA to San Francisco, stopping off en route to see, among much else, Niagara Falls, Chicago (still rising from the ashes of a devastating fire the previous year), the Rocky Mountains and Denver. From San Francisco they sailed across the Pacific to visit Japan and China. During the stay in India, Thomas was deeply moved by the visit to Serampore where his hero the renowned missionary William Carey had served. The Taj Mahal in Agra was another highlight of his stay in that country. From India the party returned to England via the Red Sea and the Suez Canal.

Such was the interest in Thomas's journey that *The Times* invited him to send regular reports for publication in the paper. Ever mindful of his Christian priorities he also sent reports to two Baptist newspapers. As he explained to readers:

> In a tour around the world, missions and missionaries constitute natural topics of thought and of conversation; indeed, I regard this subject as one of the elements of special interest to engage the attention of travellers. . . . On board the steamers of the Pacific and these Eastern seas, we are almost certain to meet with missionaries travelling to and from their fields of labour.

It is hardly surprising that Thomas, a former evangelist, should have been so passionate about the work the missionaries were doing. He was clearly inspired by those he met on his travels, writing: 'the missionary subject has presented itself to me with renewed and increased force, and I felt as though I could not but speak and write of the things I have seen and heard'. He was convinced that his missionary reports 'will be appreciated by many who laudably contribute to the support of Missionary operations, and who labour and pray for the conversion of the world to Christ'.

On his journey Thomas met two people who made a particularly deep impression on him. One was Rev. James Smith, who ran a mission station in Delhi. This clergyman was so highly esteemed that he was invited to give an address to Prince Alfred, the Duke of Edinburgh (Queen Victoria's second son), when the Prince visited Delhi. Thomas was inspired by Smith and praised him in the following way: 'I question if in Delhi there is a man more respected or who yields a more potent influence for good than the Rev. James Smith . . . with all he says his great and only teaching is to make Christ known as the only Saviour. I could not but feel how puny many revilers of Christian missions would look in the presence of such a man.'

He was also struck by the 'constant readiness for missionary work' of a Mrs Ward on board the steamer. He was impressed by 'her daily and careful teaching of one of our Chinese waiters who had learnt to read the Scriptures in San Francisco and desired a more perfect knowledge of the way to salvation, that he might be able to teach his fellow countrymen on his return to China'.

Thomas himself took advantage of any opportunity that arose on the journey to share his faith. In Chicago he gave a sermon at the Freewill Baptist Chapel and while in Benares, India, he was 'invited to the Baptist Sunday School, where I spoke words of encouragement to about seventy children and a number of actively devoted teachers'.

This first round-the-world leisure tour so captured the imagination of the public that it became an annual event. By the time of Thomas's death in 1892 almost two thousand people had circumnavigated the globe with his company, a tremendous tribute to his visionary thinking and pioneering spirit.

Rift between father and son

The same year Thomas completed his global tour, 1873, business was booming and the company opened new purpose-built headquarters in Ludgate Circus, London. John was put in charge of operations there. The company's continual growth should have been a source of great satisfaction to both father and son who, on the outside, might have seemed to form the perfect team. But, sadly, this was not the case. They had totally opposite attitudes to business and a gulf opened up between them that grew ever wider.

John was uncompromisingly profit-driven and it infuriated him that his father did not appear to treat business seriously enough, always giving priority to his religious and philanthropic activities. He was frustrated that Thomas devoted so much time and money to supporting missions around the world and visiting them as often as he could. He also fiercely objected when Thomas gave concessionary fares to Baptist parties travelling to Rome in 1875 and the United States in 1877. Thomas's joy that 'the social feeling has risen above the commercial' was something that John simply could not understand.

Writing to Marianne on 24 March 1873 from one of his tours to the Holy Land, Thomas gave his account of the rift between himself and their son:

> He does not like my mixing Missions with business but he cannot deprive me of the pleasure I have in the combination; it has sweetened my journey and I hope improved my heart without prejudice to the mercenary object of the tour. I shall neither be expelled from the office nor stifled in my spirit's utterance, and I have told him so very plainly.

John was equally direct about their business relationship: 'we never worked well together and . . . our notions of business were so opposite that I did not believe we ever could'.

But his patience finally ran out. In a letter to Thomas on 22 February 1878 he wrote:

> I state distinctly that I will not sign nor enter into any new arrangements
> for partnership with you upon any terms; all your recent letters prove the
> impossibility of us working together. . . . I . . . refer you to my repeated
> offers commencing at least three years back when I asked you to relieve
> me of a partnership which had always been irksome to me.

With the partnership agreement due to expire on 30 December 1878 John
made it clear he would not renew it. On 8 August he wrote to Thomas 'I
must be left unfettered as the sole manager' and insisted that he should have
'sole legal and monetary responsibility'. Thomas, now seventy, had just
built Thorncroft, a house on Leicester's London Road for his retirement,
and John no doubt felt that his father no longer had his mind fully on the
business anyway. And so, early in 1879, the partnership was dissolved 'by
mutual consent' and John took full control of the company.

Despite the tension between them, they clearly felt some degree of affection
and respect for each other. Thomas was always open to reconciliation and
had written to Marianne: 'I know my heart is right towards him.' Long
after the partnership with John had ended, Thomas signed a letter to him
'Your truly affectionate father'. John, too, however sharp the content of
his letters to his father, always signed them 'Your affectionate son'. He
also recognized that his father's vision and pioneering spirit had laid the
foundations on which the success of the company had been built, and his
respect for Thomas was clearly evident when he graciously wrote to him
at the time their partnership ended: 'As long as you live I want you to have
half the profits of this business.'

The tragic death of Annie

With no further involvement in the company, Thomas moved into his
retirement home in Leicester with Marianne and their daughter Annie. He
immersed himself in church and temperance work, becoming more actively
involved in the Archdeacon Lane Baptist Chapel where the family had
worshipped since the time they had first come to Leicester. Annie was a
dedicated teacher in the Sunday school with its nine hundred pupils and she
also played a key role in the young women's sewing group.

Sadly, just two years into Thomas's retirement, the family was struck
by tragedy. On Saturday, 6 November 1880, Annie returned home from
an evening meeting of the sewing group, had supper with her parents, then

about 11 p.m. went upstairs for a bath. She switched on the new gas water heater attached to the bath. Everything seemed quite normal, but in the morning something was most unusual. Each Sunday at about 7.15 a.m. Annie would take a cup of tea into her parents' room, but this Sunday she didn't. Marianne went into Annie's bedroom to see if anything was wrong and discovered she hadn't slept there. Alarmed, she informed Thomas, who immediately rushed upstairs and burst into the bathroom. To his utter horror he found Annie with her face under the water. At just thirty-five years of age she was dead.

It was subsequently found that the gas water heater was faulty and had emitted toxic fumes which caused Annie to lose consciousness and slip into the water. The official verdict at the inquest was death by drowning.

Thomas and Marianne had been very close to Annie and were inconsolable at her death. Thomas lost little time in deciding how to honour her memory. Annie herself had drawn his attention to a piece of land opposite Archdeacon Lane Chapel which she felt would be ideal for erecting a building for the Sunday school. Only a week after her funeral a letter from him was published in the *Leicester Chronicle* stating his intention to do just that. The Annie Cook Memorial Hall and Sunday School Room were duly opened less than two years later on 30 April 1882. Among other things in his speech, Thomas stated that the hall would be for general hire but would not be let for 'any object which was avowedly hostile to the principles of the Christian religion'. Both alcohol and smoking would be forbidden.

Marianne never got over Annie's death and in the course of the next three and a half years her health gradually declined. Thomas took her to various spa and seaside resorts but these had no effect. Her last year, Thomas wrote, was one of 'extreme trial' and on 8 March 1884 she died, aged seventy-seven. She was laid to rest with Annie in Leicester's Welford Road Cemetery.

The death and legacy of Thomas Cook

After the loss of Marianne, loneliness was a heavy cross for Thomas to bear. However, he found great strength in his faith and took comfort from his favourite hymn, 'Forever with the Lord'. The words in that hymn 'Be Thou at my right hand, / Then can I never fail; / Uphold Thou me, and I shall stand, / Fight, and I must prevail' were no doubt a great encouragement to him.

Despite his bereavements, Thomas remained positive and active. Even after turning eighty, when he became increasingly frail and blind, he continued to attend temperance meetings and to travel, and when he was completely blind he actually travelled to the Holy Land. His last public act was to unveil a block of almshouses and a mission hall in 1891 in his home village of Melbourne in memory of his beloved wife and daughter. In addition to the loving bond he had enjoyed with them, they had faithfully supported him in all his business activities and frequently accompanied him on his excursions. Annie, a fluent French speaker, often acted as his interpreter.

But eventually his frailty caught up with him and when the end came, it came out of the blue. About 8 p.m. on 18 July 1892 he was having supper at home when he suddenly felt unwell with a severe pain in his side. The doctor was called but could do nothing to help. Three hours later Thomas, aged eighty-three, was dead. He had suffered a fatal stroke.

The Archdeacon Lane Baptist Chapel was full to overflowing for his funeral service. The hearse carrying his coffin was pulled to Leicester's Welford Road Cemetery by six black horses bedecked with plumes of black feathers. They were followed by the Mayor of Leicester at the head of a procession of twelve horse-drawn carriages. Flags in Leicester were flown at half-mast. In the cemetery itself a great crowd was present when Thomas was laid to rest with Marianne and Annie.

In its obituary the *Leicester Daily Post* quoted the praise expressed for Thomas the previous year by William Gladstone, four-times British Prime Minister, when the company celebrated its fiftieth anniversary: 'Thousands and thousands of the inhabitants of these islands who never would for a moment have passed beyond its shores, have been able to go and return in safety and comfort, and with great enjoyment, great refreshment and great improvement to themselves.' Even before then Gladstone had already proclaimed that through Cook's tours 'whole classes have, for the first time, found easy access to foreign countries, and have acquired some of that familiarity with them which breeds not contempt but kindness'.

It would have given Thomas great joy to know that his tours had helped bring 'man nearer to man'. He would also have been delighted that he had helped bring man 'nearer to his Creator' by making accessible 'God's earth with all its fullness and beauty' to countless millions. It is easy to understand, therefore, why William Gladstone esteemed him so highly and ranked him among the nation's great 'public benefactors'. Like Gladstone, we can all admire Thomas Cook for his remarkable achievements and we can be grateful to him for the gift of affordable leisure travel he gave to the world.

HENRY CROWELL
and the story of Quaker Oats

The happy, smiling image of a man in Quaker clothing is one of the most recognized logos in the world. His face instantly calls to mind a breakfast cereal enjoyed by millions. This popular cereal is, however, only one of many food products marketed under the name Quaker Oats, a giant company established by a man of exceptional character who refused to allow a life-threatening medical condition, heart-breaking personal tragedy and ferocious opposition to defeat him.

His name is Henry Parsons Crowell. His story is remarkable and has many twists and turns. Even the name of his company is a surprise because neither he nor it ever had any connection with the Quaker faith.

Early life

Henry Parsons Crowell was born to Luther and Anna Crowell in Cleveland, Ohio, on 27 January 1855. He was the first of their three children, all boys. The boys grew up in a comfortable home as Luther was co-owner of a successful wholesale shoe business in the town. It was also a warm, Christian home. The family worshipped at the Second Presbyterian Church in Cleveland.

Throughout his life Luther had suffered with tuberculosis. By the time he was thirty-five his condition had considerably deteriorated and after learning there was no cure, he set up a trust fund for Anna to ensure the financial security of the family and provide an inheritance for the boys. He lingered on another four years and was eventually permanently confined to bed. On 20 November 1864 at the age of thirty-nine he died in the family home.

Finding faith

The pastor of their church, Dr Theron Hawks, came over to comfort the three boys at Luther's graveside on the day of the funeral. Henry, in distress, immediately asked if he could meet with him. He was only nine years old and was frightened and desperately wanted to talk to someone.

The morning after the funeral he met with Dr Hawks in his study and poured out his heart to him. He couldn't come to terms with the loss of his father and wanted to know if he would see him again in heaven. His burning question was, how could he be sure that he himself would be going there? Dr Hawks slowly and sensitively explained to him that Jesus Christ had opened the way to heaven for anyone who accepted His gift of eternal life. He explained that a person's sinful nature was put to death with Jesus on the cross and that He invites us to live in relationship with Him in the power of His resurrection.

Young though he was, Henry felt the power of those words. They penetrated into the very depths of his being and he at once invited Jesus into his life. It was not a spur-of-the-moment, emotional reaction prompted by a deep sense of personal loss. He always acknowledged this as the moment when his lifelong Christian faith was born.

Schooldays

In anticipation of his death Luther had asked Anna's thirty-four-year-old brother, Joel Parsons, to become the guardian of his three sons. Joel readily agreed and when he later married, his wife also joined the household. Henry formed a close bond with his uncle and learned much from him about history, politics and current affairs. Joel also convinced Henry of the importance of a good education and suggested, with Anna's full support, that he should aim for entry to Yale. The first step was to find a suitable school.

It was Henry's good friend Howard Eells who pointed him to the Greylock Institute. He was a pupil at this private boarding school for a thousand boys near Williamstown, Massachusetts, and constantly sang its praises. He told Henry it was in beautiful countryside with excellent fishing opportunities and had impressive sports facilities and dedicated teachers. He particularly singled out the president, Dr Benjamin Mills, a devout Christian who treated each boy as a valued member of his family. Dr Mills frequently remarked: 'To me, every boy is a prayerful study and

I constantly seek the help of the Lord in dealing with them. Every boy is a member of my home.'

Henry was persuaded by Howard's infectious enthusiasm and in the autumn of 1867, aged twelve, enrolled for the start of the new term. Greylock was to be his second home for the next five years.

During his time there he came to look upon Dr Mills as a surrogate father. He was greatly impressed by the genuine love and care Dr Mills showed for all the boys in his charge. He was an attentive listener always ready to give sound advice. Interviewed in later life about his schooldays, Henry said: 'I was never a brilliant student. I was athletically inclined. Thoroughly enjoyed the gym. I was good at baseball, a leader in athletics, and pretty well developed. Greylock was a beautiful Christian school and meant everything to me. The teachers were such earnest Christians, especially President Mills. He has been a great influence over my life for seventy-five years.'

Tuberculosis strikes again

Henry's time at Greylock came to a premature end when, tragically, the school burned down in April 1872 and all the boys were sent home. They were told to return in the autumn when the building would again be ready for use. But Henry was never to return.

He had enjoyed robust good health in his first three years at the school but over the next two years he was increasingly troubled by an irritating cough. He also began to lose weight. Despite this he happily helped out in the family shoe business while back home. Just before the start of the autumn term he went to the family doctor for a check-up and was delivered a shattering blow: he was told he had tuberculosis just like his father. He had to leave school immediately.

None of the family knew that all three of Luther's sons had inherited their father's medical condition. As there was no cure at the time, the doctor's statement was a death sentence. Sadly, Henry's two brothers were to die of the illness, Edward at twenty-eight, Charles at thirty-nine.

Henry was distraught to learn of his condition but was given a glimmer of hope when the doctor explained that medicine had progressed since his father's death and some doctors now believed that the illness could be stopped by outdoor life in a friendly climate. Even so, it could take up to ten years for this to happen.

Inspired by D. L. Moody

During this black period Henry spent much time reading the Bible. His faith was given a significant boost in the spring of 1873 when the renowned evangelist Dwight L. Moody was invited to speak at his church. Moody, in his address, quoted what he had once been told by a man named Henry Varley: 'The world has yet to see what God can do with and for and through and in any man who is fully consecrated to Him.' Moody explained how those words had challenged him: 'Varley meant any man! Well, with the Holy Spirit in me, I'll be one of those men!'

Henry was profoundly moved by what he heard:

> Moody's words were the words of the Lord to me. I saw now that the wrecking of my school plans didn't really matter. God didn't need His men educated, or brilliant, or anything else! All God needed was just a man! Well by the grace of God, I would be God's man! To be sure, I would never preach like Moody but I could make money and help support the labours of men like Moody. Then I resolved, 'Oh God, if You will allow me to make money to be used in Your service I will keep my name out of it so You will have the glory.'

He was so overwhelmed with emotion that he had to slip out of the church to take it all in.

Declining health

Henry's correspondence at the time reveals deep joy and a hunger for 'a deeper, clearer view of Him who is the Creator and Inspirer of us all'. However, his deepening spirituality was not accompanied by any improvement in his health. By August 1874 it had declined to such an extent that he was almost permanently confined to bed. The situation looked hopeless. All the signs suggested that he would suffer the same fate as his father.

During his Bible reading in the long hours in bed he became increasingly aware of how often the number seven occurred. On one particular occasion, reading Job 5:19, the words struck him as if they had been written just for him: 'He shall deliver you in six troubles, yes, in seven no evil shall touch you.' He felt that God was telling him that his lung condition would continue for another six years but that it would not be fatal. He would be free of it in the seventh year. This lifted his spirits and gave him renewed hope.

Ironically, after the encouragement of those uplifting words, his condition deteriorated and reached the critical stage. But he hung on to what he had read in Job 5:19, convinced that this was not the end. His conviction was reinforced when his doctor told him he had to live outdoors for the next seven years in a more moderate climate to have any hope of survival. The specific mention of the number seven struck Henry as confirmation of the promise God had made to him.

Ranch work in Colorado

With a move away from Cleveland essential for his health the question was where to go. Family friends who had just returned from a trip to Colorado suggested that the climate there—cool summers and mild winters with plenty of sunshine—would be ideal for him.

And so, in September 1874, aged nineteen, Henry left for Denver, a small town in Colorado with a population of just six thousand close to the Rocky Mountains. He had regained enough strength to be able to travel on his own and to look after himself on arrival. The money his father had left him ensured that he could live comfortably.

On arrival in Denver he checked into the Inter Ocean, the town's only hotel. As he entered the dining room for breakfast next morning, he was amazed to see an old friend from Cleveland, George Worthington, sitting there. George, like himself, had come to Denver on medical advice because he, too, was suffering from tuberculosis.

George told him he had discovered a ranch where he could work outdoors in return for board and lodging and suggested that Henry should join him. Henry agreed and for almost a year the friends enjoyed life on the Colorado ranch. However, by the summer both were homesick and decided to spend a short time in Cleveland before going back to the ranch in September.

While in Cleveland Henry went to see the family doctor and was encouraged to hear that there had been an improvement in his condition. Clearly, outdoor work in a kinder climate was proving beneficial. However, the doctor stressed it would take several more years before any talk of being cured was possible.

Meeting Lillie Wick

During that summer of 1875 Henry was struck one Sunday at church by the sight of a very attractive teenager. Her name was Lillie Wick. He had last seen her when she was twelve and he was amazed at the change in her. Now fifteen, she had returned with her family from Germany where she had been attending school.

They saw each other several times and became quite close but in September they had to go their separate ways, Henry to Colorado and Lillie back to school. But their paths would cross again.

To California

Henry and George did not, in fact, return to Colorado as originally intended but at the last minute decided to explore California on horseback instead. Over the next few months they covered several hundred miles of trail, sometimes across very difficult mountain terrain. They then returned to Cleveland for a summer break.

Henry's main reason for returning was to see Lillie Wick. He didn't realize how much he had missed her and it was clear the feeling was mutual. It was magical to be together during those summer weeks but all too quickly the time sped by and they had to separate again. They accepted that Henry had to return to the friendlier California climate for the sake of his health and that they would have to rely on letters to share their feelings.

In the following months it was apparent that Henry's health had radically improved. He and George managed to keep up a gruelling physical schedule which, in view of their condition, almost defies imagination. The conquest of the formidable Half Dome, a massive rock in the Yosemite Valley in the Sierra Nevada mountains that had beaten many other climbers, was just one of their remarkable achievements.

Engagement to Lillie Wick

Henry was excited that he seemed to be winning the battle with his illness and he desperately wanted confirmation. In the summer of 1877 he travelled to Philadelphia to see Dr Silas Weir Mitchell, a specialist in tuberculosis, hoping to hear good news. Dr Mitchell's assessment was hugely encouraging.

He assured Henry that there had, indeed, been a significant improvement in his health and that he could afford to be optimistic. He stressed, however, that the battle was by no means over and another three years of outdoor life were essential.

All this was music to Henry's ears. Surely he could now make long-term plans for Lillie and himself? They both knew they wanted to spend the rest of their lives together but hadn't dared believe it possible because of his tuberculosis. He told Lillie the good news and promptly proposed to her. Lillie accepted and they immediately announced their engagement.

Storm clouds

Henry then returned to California. By spring 1878 he was on his own as George had fully recovered his health and taken up a position in business. Wondering whether to stay or not, Henry happened to meet a man who told him about a new town in North Dakota called Fargo at the heart of vast tracts of land ideal for farming. This news triggered Henry's entrepreneurial instincts. Seeing the potential for a farming business there he decided to leave California and explore the area. But he had to put his plans on hold after receiving a distressing letter from Lillie. She wrote:

> Our engagement has given my mother great sorrow. She insists that I break off with you. I do not know what to do, as I cannot bear to hurt her. Since Father died, she is so lonely. She fears that your fate is the same as that of my father; that you will not live to raise a family and care for your wife. She does not want me to be left a widow as she was. I wish you were here to advise me.

This was shattering news. Henry wrote to Mrs Wick explaining that Dr Mitchell had made a very positive assessment of his health. He also told her about the assurance he had received from his reading of Job 5:19. None of this made the slightest difference. Mrs Wick remained firm. The engagement must end.

Henry thought he might be able to change her mind if she could see for herself how well he looked. He therefore returned to Cleveland to meet with her. It was pointless. Mrs Wick was determined to spare her daughter the heartbreak of an early bereavement. Henry was devastated. There was nothing more he could do. His only hope was that Mrs Wick might, in time, come to see things differently. Heartbroken, he left Cleveland and headed for Fargo.

Any lingering hope he may have had was finally shattered when he received another letter from Lillie shortly after his departure:

> Please know that my love for you is great, but my duty is clear. I must act in accordance with the wishes of my dear mother and thereby ease her grief and despair. I accept the full responsibility for not thinking how she has been troubled deeply by Father's death, and does not wish her daughter to have a similar calamity befall her. With a crushed heart and out of concern for the grief of my mother, I must regretfully break our engagement.

Farming in Fargo

Somehow Henry had to pick himself up and get on with life. He prayed earnestly about what to do next. He felt that, in answer to his prayer, God was guiding him to act on his entrepreneurial instincts and buy a thousand-acre stretch of farmland twelve miles south of Fargo with money from his inheritance. Henry bought the land and set to work erecting a barn, ploughing fields and planting wheat. At harvest time he hired reapers to help him cut and stack the healthy crop he had grown. A promising business was under way.

But one day, quite unexpectedly, he thought he had lost everything. He was heading to Fargo when he caught sight of a tornado twisting and spiralling towards his farm. Afraid of being caught in its path, he raced his horse and buggy to the town. Thankfully he was not hit.

The next morning he returned to the farm to survey the damage. On the way he saw property in ruins, sheaves of wheat lying scattered around for miles and clothing hanging in tree tops. He feared the worst for his own farm, fully expecting it to be wrecked, but on arrival he could hardly believe his eyes. Everything was still intact. None of the buildings had been damaged and all the sheaves of wheat were still in place. Even the farmhands were carrying on work as usual.

He was staggered. He firmly believed that God had spared his farm but had no idea why. The answer arrived soon after when out of the blue a Fargo real estate agent informed him that someone was keen to buy it.

Henry felt that God was prompting him to move on from the farm and he promptly sold it.

Breeding draught horses

However, he was keen to continue farming elsewhere and when he learned that a 17,000-acre tract of land was available near the Red River about fifty miles south of Fargo he bought it. His initial plan was to plant wheat but after a conversation with an uncle who was a breeder of Percheron horses, he decided to breed them himself. He knew he had a ready market as there was great demand from farmers in the area for quality draught horses for ploughing.

By spring 1879, just six months after buying the land, he had erected all the necessary buildings to accommodate good breeding stock. With his uncle's guidance he bought three hundred mares and a stallion in Ohio and chartered a special train to transport them from Cleveland to Fargo.

With a natural flair for marketing, Henry had giant signs painted on the sides of the wagons boldly displaying the words 'The Red River Percheron Parade'. Amazed onlookers stopped to stare along the 850-mile route and, by the time the train had reached Fargo, word of the Percherons had spread throughout the area.

Lillie Wick: renewed hope

When Henry came to Cleveland with his cargo of horses he paid a visit to Lillie and Mrs Wick. Although he and Lillie had officially broken off their engagement, their feelings for each other remained strong and they had kept in touch by letter. Lillie and Mrs Wick were amazed when they saw Henry. He looked in such robust health. Lillie could see no reason, therefore, why they should not be engaged and wrote to Dr Mitchell in Philadelphia to ask his opinion:

> When we were engaged, Mr Crowell being then so delicate, Mama feared his recovery to perfect health impossible, and the idea of her dying and leaving her only child with an invalid husband drove her to despair. Knowing the trouble she has passed through, and with the desire to lighten this last burden, I sacrificed the fondest hope of my life and broke the engagement. But Mr Crowell returned to Cleveland, April 21, with so decided an improvement in every respect that both Mama and I are

greatly encouraged. Hope revived! Do you think Mr Crowell's health will ever permit our hope to be realized?

Dr Mitchell replied that it was far too soon to talk of marriage and explained that Henry would need to spend another two or three years outdoors before any final decision could be made. The couple respected his opinion. They were prepared to wait.

Cured at last

In the spring of 1881 Henry decided to diversify and planted 2,500 of his 17,000 acres with wheat. As the wheat began to grow it looked strong and healthy and there was every sign of a bumper harvest. But then disaster struck. A three-day spell of exceptionally hot weather caused it to shrivel and the crop was ruined.

Henry was puzzled. He had asked God for guidance before buying the farm and was sure this was where he had been led. What was God saying to him now? As before when he had asked this question a buyer appeared out of the blue with a very good offer. Henry was convinced this was more than just coincidence. He could see a pattern and felt sure God wanted him to move on again.

It proved to be perfect timing. After a further examination by Dr Mitchell he received the news he had worked for and dreamt of during the past seven years: he was completely cured of tuberculosis! He no longer needed to stay on the farm and work outdoors because the whole world was now open to him. He could go anywhere he wanted. It was exactly as God had promised in Job 5:19.

The Quaker Mill at Ravenna

The next step was not clear but of one thing Henry was certain: growing crops was not for him. His two experiences of farming had convinced him that it was too weather-dependent and that he should look for something over which he could have greater control. Upon selling the farm he returned to Cleveland, confident that God would show him the way forward.

Not long after his return he learned that an oat milling business based at the Quaker Mill in Ravenna, forty miles from Cleveland, was for sale.

Although he had no experience of this occupation he was strangely drawn to the mill and in November 1881 bought it. He explained why:

> When I heard about this, I immediately thought: This is probably what God has planned for me. I had been seven years in search of health, and health was found. It was apparent that I no longer was obliged to live out-of-doors; I was ready for indoor life and work. I could not help reviewing the whole affair in my mind, and when I did, the hand of God was evident in every part of it. As I grew better and became well, God evidently did not want me to be a farmer. He took me out of one farm by a tornado and out of the second by a hot wind. And now that the seven years were finished, He was opening the way for me to secure the Quaker mill. I felt compelled to go to my room. There, for a long time, I thanked Him for all His blessings.

Ferdinand Schumacher, 'The Oatmeal King'

Henry, now twenty-six, could never have foreseen that in buying the mill he had taken a significant step on a path to unimaginable success and wealth. This would have seemed highly improbable at the time because oats were not considered fit for human consumption. They were eaten only in Scotland and pockets of Germany and Ireland and were considered primarily to be horse fodder. In fact, the English derided their Scottish neighbours for 'robbing the ponies'.

It was a German immigrant to the United States, Ferdinand Schumacher, who transformed the perception of oatmeal. It was very popular in his home area in Germany as an edible food product and he thought it would be worth trying to sell it in his grocery store in Akron, Ohio. His sales were so good that he bought an old woollen mill in Akron and turned it over to oatmeal production to meet the rising demand. He soon established a reputation as an oatmeal producer and earned the nickname 'The Oatmeal King'.

Success with the Quaker Mill

The mill Henry had bought had no connection whatsoever with the Quaker faith, despite its name. The four partners who had started the original oatmeal business at the mill in 1877 called themselves the Quaker Mill Company merely as a marketing ploy. Quakers were associated with purity and integrity and the partners felt the name Quaker in the company's title would create customer confidence in their product. To further reinforce the positive association with Quakers they adopted as the company's logo the figure of a Quaker man holding a scroll with the word 'Pure' written across it.

However, despite their best efforts, their business failed after two years and was sold. The next owner also ran it for two years under the same name but he, too, could not make a success of it and sold it to Henry.

Although the Quaker name and logo had not prevented the failure of the two previous milling companies, Henry retained them. As a Christian, he fully identified with the values of purity and integrity that they represented.

He was excited about his new venture and even at this early stage felt he had found his niche. His first step was to persuade a relative of his age, James Andrews, to join him in partnership. James had considerable technical knowledge and skill and took charge of production. Henry oversaw administration and marketing. Within just a year this enterprising pair had achieved such good sales because of the quality of their product that competitors began to look nervously in their direction.

Joy—and heartbreak

With his health fully restored and with a promising business under way Henry felt this was the ideal time to ask Lillie to marry him. Mrs Wick was no longer opposed and in November 1881 allowed them to renew their engagement. Their long wait and hard struggle were finally over. They were married on 29 June 1882 in the home of Lillie's Uncle Charles and Aunt Cynthia in Cleveland in a ceremony conducted by the pastor of the Second Presbyterian Church. This was truly a day to celebrate.

The newly married couple initially made their home in Ravenna but several months later returned to Cleveland to live with Henry's mother pending the birth of their daughter, Annie. She was born on 3 May 1883. They then took an apartment in the Stillman Hotel, Cleveland, from where Henry commuted to his mill in Ravenna. They were blissfully happy.

But tragically and unexpectedly, their happiness was cut short. Early in January 1885 Lillie began to feel very unwell and had to take to her bed. She had caught a virulent strain of influenza and grew rapidly weaker. Henry was alarmed. The doctor gave her medication but it had no effect. Henry stayed by Lillie's bedside day and night holding her hand and wiping the perspiration from her brow. But on 10 January her battle with the illness was lost. She died in their Cleveland apartment aged just twenty-four. She was laid to rest in Lake View Cemetery.

Henry was inconsolable. He never forgot Lillie. For the next sixty years he carried in his waistcoat pocket the little gold chain that had been attached to her watch. Just a few days before he died he placed it in the Chicago vault where his most valuable documents were safely kept.

He could not have managed without the support of Mrs Wick who recognized the tragic irony of his situation. She had pressured Lillie into breaking off her engagement to spare her the pain of a premature bereavement only for Henry to suffer this fate. She looked after him like a mother, comforting him, ensuring that he did not go without meals and, above all, taking care of Annie. At that time it would have been unthinkable for a working man to bring up a child alone and so Mrs Wick cared for her in her own home until her marriage. Henry, of course, was always there for Annie and they were very close. In later years he became a doting grandfather to her four children.

The failed consortium

Following Lillie's death Henry threw himself into his work. As new mills began to appear, oatmeal production began to outstrip demand and fierce competition developed among millers. Despite the fact that his own business was thriving, Henry unselfishly proposed the formation of a consortium of all twenty-one millers east of the Rocky Mountains to work together for the benefit of all.

His idea was to operate under a single trade name, fix a minimum price below which no mill would sell and adopt a common marketing policy. All but Ferdinand Schumacher, the country's leading oatmeal producer, joined. He saw no need to protect his interests in this way, fully convinced that his name alone would guarantee a profitable business.

In 1886 the Oatmeal Millers' Association was duly formed but despite its good intentions its life was short. Some of its greedier members, disregarding the agreement, undercut the others. The penalties imposed proved to be no deterrent and the Association collapsed after just a few months.

Chapter 3

Another try

However, Henry and twelve other millers were prepared to try again. This time Schumacher reluctantly joined the group because he had come to recognize how well some of his competitors were doing and feared a genuine threat to his domination of the field.

The agreement reached was that each of the member mills would sell at a fixed price, operate within a specified area and receive a percentage of the consortium's profits in direct proportion to its production capacity.

On 4 May 1887 the new combination was incorporated as the Consolidated Oatmeal Company. Henry was elected president, his good friend Robert Stuart vice-president and Schumacher treasurer.

It stung sixty-five-year-old Schumacher that Henry—in his view a young, inexperienced upstart—was elected president instead of himself. It gnawed at him that the other millers held him in such high regard. It was the start of deepening resentment towards him.

A new love

Henry's involvement in the oat milling business had helped to distract him from the loneliness he felt after Lillie's death. Friends and colleagues, too, did what they could to try to fill the gap. One couple in particular, Ned and Rose Murfey, played a key part in helping him find happiness again.

Henry had been a regular dinner guest at their home and one evening in April 1888 they invited a lifelong friend of Rose, twenty-eight-year-old Susan Coleman, to join them. Susan, a Latin and Maths teacher, had just returned from a period of study in Germany. She and Henry hit it off immediately and began to dine with the Murfeys on a regular basis. They grew closer. Henry was struck not only by Susan's beauty but also by her sharp intelligence, good humour and amazing grasp of business matters. She often saw a solution to a work-related problem that others did not.

They were soon spending all their free time together. After just three months they were so sure they wanted to spend the rest of their lives together that they married at Susan's home in Cleveland on 10 July 1888. The ceremony was conducted by the Rev. Henry Aves, minister of St John's Episcopal Church where her family worshipped. They spent their first few weeks as a married couple with the Murfeys in Ravenna but in the autumn moved to Chicago when the Consolidated Oatmeal Company relocated its headquarters there.

Collapse of the Consolidated Oatmeal Company

Henry and Susan may well have wondered why they had bothered to move because Consolidated soon ran into trouble.

As new mills began to appear the company bought them up or leased them to try to fend off competition. Unscrupulous speculators were quick to exploit the situation by erecting mills as an investment, knowing that Consolidated would want to acquire them. In one extreme case a speculator was paid an annual fee for agreeing not to build any mills at all. More than half the company's profits were lost through these futile attempts to maintain their market position. But the situation was made worse when some of the group's members began to undercut the others.

Knowing Consolidated was doomed, seven of the group, among them Henry and Schumacher, decided to try yet another pooling arrangement and formed a holding company, the American Cereal Company, which was chartered in West Virginia in December 1888.

A lucrative sideline

Meanwhile, amid all the chaos in the oat milling business, Henry became involved in another commercial venture when Susan convinced him that an assistant in a Cleveland hardware store, Frank Drury, had a business idea worth backing.

Drury had bought the rights to a new kind of oil stove that combined heating and cooking functions. It was selling well but he didn't have the capital to increase production. As people were moving in ever-growing numbers into the cities, Susan could see the need for a small product like this in apartments that were not big enough for a wood-burning stove.

Henry and Drury met and agreed to form a partnership. They acquired the disused buildings of an old factory and set up the Cleveland Foundry Company with a workforce of thirty-six. Their sales figures in the first two years were impressive and led them to add to their product range by manufacturing stoves with different burner sizes.

Their company took a gigantic leap forward when John D. Rockefeller, creator of the Standard Oil Company, approached them with an inspired idea. He was concerned at the huge lakes of kerosene (paraffin) that he accumulated in the oil refining process, a waste product for which there was no market. He offered to put his three thousand salesmen at Cleveland Foundry's disposal and sell their stoves if they would use kerosene to fuel them.

Collaboration followed and, as Rockefeller had predicted, demand for both the stoves and the kerosene rocketed. The sales made Henry and Drury millionaires and the Cleveland Foundry—later called the Perfection Stove Company—became the world's largest producer of stoves.

Henry was much loved by the workforce at the factory. Despite his reputation for firmness, he was also known for his warmth, kindness, patience and humility. He had a word for everyone. A later president of the company, who had seen the way he treated people, remarked: 'I'm not much of a churchman but I can go for Mr Crowell's type of Christianity.'

Schumacher gains control

Although involved with the stove business Henry did not neglect his milling interests and firmly hoped that American Cereal would achieve the success that had eluded the earlier pooling arrangements. However, Schumacher made things difficult from the start.

It had been agreed that the millers who produced more than one variety of grain would invest the profits from all their milling operations in the holding. However, Schumacher had been allowed to submit the profits from his oatmeal operation only. When it came to light that he was assigning most of his overheads to oatmeal production alone so as to show a reduced profit in this operation, it caused great anger and members threatened to pull out if he didn't fall into line.

Somehow Henry and Stuart managed to persuade them all, including Schumacher, that the way forward was to convert the holding company into a single operating company. Profits from all milling activities across the group would be invested in it. Formal integration was agreed and the group was incorporated as the American Cereal Company of Ohio on 1 June 1891.

Conscious that the three previous attempts at cooperation had failed through some millers' lack of integrity, Henry was determined to establish an ethical basis for the company and insisted this should be formally incorporated into the policy document. Accordingly, it was agreed 'That our selling organization should consist of men who were honest, intelligent, of good character and . . . willing to render the very best of service to the customers. Our purpose was not only to give to the customers the very best of cereals but to render to the jobbers [wholesalers] and retailer a service that could not be equalled.'

After incorporation there was an immediate shift in the balance of power. Henry and Stuart each received 12 per cent of the stock and bonds for their respective plants whereas Schumacher received over 50 per cent. With overall control he was elected president. Henry was appointed vice-president, Stuart secretary-treasurer.

Battle begins

A major decision taken in the first twelve months was to centralize production and reduce operating costs by closing down some of the plants. It was agreed that Schumacher's plant in Akron should become the hub of operations because of its excellent location and capacity for expansion. It was further agreed that Quaker Oats, because of its outstanding sales success, should be the group's flagship product. In just a decade Henry had increased the value of his business from $25,000 when he bought it to over $500,000 (in today's values, from $690,000 to $14 million). He recognized, however, that further growth was only possible by moving his operation in Ravenna to the larger, more practical plant at Akron.

There was a considerable degree of harmony in the operating company's first six years and excellent profits were made, but then cracks began to appear. It became obvious that Henry and Schumacher were on a collision course.

Henry was concerned that storing oatmeal in open barrels was unhygienic. It was an easy target for insects and vermin; even the occasional cat was known to curl up in the soft, comfortable oats. He pushed for packaging in clean, attractive cartons. Schumacher was violently opposed to this, considering it an unnecessary expense.

Schumacher was also hostile to Henry's marketing ideas, dismissing them as gimmicks. Henry was promoting Quaker Oats everywhere—in newspapers, store windows, trams, on posters, at trade fairs and exhibitions, on the sides of railway wagons, on fences in country roads. He also gave away free samples in major cities. Recalling the success of the Red River

Percheron Parade, he chartered a freight train from Cedar Rapids, Iowa, to Portland on the Pacific coast. The wagons boldly displayed posters of giant cereal packets featuring a man in Quaker clothing and the prominently displayed words 'Quaker Oats, the World's Breakfast'. In Portland itself he ensured that a sample half-ounce box of Quaker Oats was deposited in every mailbox.

This blanket saturation, reinforced by the appeal of the clean, attractive packaging, created such a demand for Quaker Oats that by 1895 annual turnover had increased to a staggering $18 million dollars ($½ billion today). Henry felt this fully justified the investment in advertising but Schumacher refused to accept this. He claimed the sales figures would have been achieved anyway, simply by word-of-mouth recommendation. He raged: 'Crowell is crazy! The grocers don't want packages, and the people don't want it neither. This advertising is silly business! We'll save our money; let our competitors advertise.'

Schumacher began to think of ways of getting rid of both Henry and Stuart. His opportunity came in 1896. The first half of that year showed an operating loss after heavy investments in grain and construction costs. Despite the fact that the deficit was overturned and the final figures for the year showed a healthy profit, Schumacher proposed at the AGM in February 1897 that Stuart, as treasurer, should resign. Because of his voting power he had little trouble in getting this proposal through.

Next he targeted Henry. Schumacher informed investors that he had lost patience with Crowell's hare-brained advertising ideas and accused him of being pushy, always wanting his own way. In advance of the 1898 AGM, Henry wrote to the directors presenting an entirely different picture. He accused Schumacher of wanting Stuart removed so that he could replace him as company treasurer with his own son, Hugo. Henry further explained it was the Quaker brand that had enabled the company to maintain its strong financial position. This surely confirmed the value of advertising. But his arguments fell on deaf ears. He was voted out.

A silver lining

Henry now found himself in the wilderness. A very black cloud hung over him but it had a silver lining—it prompted him to face up to a void within himself. Despite his regular church attendance and his assurance that God had always been guiding him, he admitted to Susan that he felt empty. He hungered for a deeper experience of God. Susan suggested they should hold a weekly Bible study at their home and invite Dr William Newell, a renowned Bible scholar, to lead it.

The studies started in the autumn of 1898 and their effect on Henry was profound. They released new spiritual energy within him and his relationship with Christ was transformed. He had a new focus: 'If my life can always be lived so as to please Him, I'll be supremely happy.'

Previously reticent about his faith, he couldn't keep the good news of Christ's life-changing power to himself and began to share it with his business associates. Many came to faith. One of them, Chicago businessman William Robinson, recalled a lunchtime conversation with him: 'One by one my objections fell away before Crowell's unanswerable presentation. I, then and there, decided, just as I would a corporate question, to come to God. From that day I have been a new creature in Christ Jesus.'

Henry's financial support for worthy causes, although always generous, now increased astronomically and for the rest of his life he donated at least 65 per cent of his gross annual income to them. These included missions and missionaries, prison ministries, Bible translations and help for the poor, for orphans and for widows.

As a result of Dr Newell's inspiring exposition of the Bible, Susan, too, was transformed. She recognized that she was merely a nominal Christian and that her church attendance was a matter of habit not heart. She saw for the first time that her sinful nature had been crucified with Christ on the cross and that she could enjoy a new life, united with Him, in the power of His resurrection.

She had previously been caught up in the mad social whirl of the Gilded 400, the exclusive set of Chicago's most wealthy and famous families, but now she became actively involved in church life and concentrated her energies on helping people and sharing the good news of Jesus Christ.

Crowell and Stuart reinstated

The upturn in Henry's spiritual life was followed by an upturn on the business front. With the departure of Crowell and Stuart the American Cereal Company had lost two of its most capable men and became rocked by internal strife. Sensing an opportunity to take advantage of its falling share prices, a syndicate of Cleveland entrepreneurs bought up stock. As a result share prices began to rise again and Schumacher, in need of money after heavy losses in another venture, sold three thousand of his. In doing so he lost overall control of the company to the syndicate.

This was the cue to invite Henry and Stuart to rejoin. At the 1899 AGM, Henry was voted in as president, Stuart as treasurer. But Henry was aware that the syndicate had an ulterior motive in taking over the company: to buy up or squeeze out all rivals and have the market to themselves, leaving them free to charge whatever prices they liked. In his address to the AGM Henry vigorously opposed their intentions on moral grounds. Furthermore, he pointed out, the company would face constant legal battles with the US government on charges of monopolistic practice.

He presented his views calmly and quietly, looking people straight in the eye. It was a tense moment. He risked being sidelined again but he had meant it when he said 'If my life can always be lived so as to please Him, I'll be supremely happy.' It was not the syndicate he felt answerable to.

Incredibly, the syndicators accepted the moral and logical force of his arguments and made no attempt to oust him. In a surprise move, realizing they could not continue the company along Henry's lines, they sold their shares and left to pursue other interests. American Cereal was now in the hands of Henry and Stuart.

Schumacher leaves the scene

But what of Schumacher? Now aged seventy-three, he was battle weary and had no more stomach for a fight. He decided to call it a day. He still owned a substantial amount of stock but hung on to it until share prices rose even higher. He then retired to enjoy a second marriage and the peace and quiet of his home in Akron.

American Cereal becomes Quaker Oats

Free to do things their way, Henry and Stuart improved production methods, promoted packaging across the board and pursued a vigorous policy of selling abroad. American Cereal thrived.

It was the highly respected Quaker Oats brand that was driving the company's huge profits and it was decided, therefore, to capitalize on the name. And so, on 20 September 1901, American Cereal was incorporated as the Quaker Oats Company, a holding company, with Henry as president and Stuart as secretary and treasurer.

To the rescue of the Moody Bible Institute

The year 1901 was a landmark one for Quaker Oats but it was also a significant year for Henry in two other ways. The first was a fire that totally destroyed his home in Rush Street, Chicago. He and Susan decided to leave the district and move with their four-year-old son Henry Junior to Winnetka, a smart northern suburb. The second was the start of an association with the Moody Bible Institute in Chicago that was to last for the rest of his life.

The Institute trained Christian ministers and missionaries. It had been founded as the Chicago Evangelization Society in 1886 by Dwight L. Moody, the famous evangelist who, it will be recalled, had so inspired eighteen-year-old Henry. The Institute was given its present name after Moody's death in 1899.

By 1901 it was in serious financial trouble and in danger of closing. At Dr William Newell's request, Henry met the trustees to offer advice. He quickly recognized that they were men of spiritual substance but without business acumen or organizational skills, and he immediately offered his services free of charge. His offer was gratefully accepted and on 24 April 1901 he was elected to the Board of Trustees.

His involvement made a radical difference. He injected a considerable amount of his own money into the Institute, set up a network of financial backers and restructured the administration to make it cost-efficient. In 1904 he was elected President of the Board and in 1907 Chairman of the Executive Committee. Right up until the time of his death forty years later he rarely missed the Executive Committee's weekly meeting.

Not only did he give the Institute a solid financial base, a clear organizational structure and sound leadership, he also set up the Moody Press, a dynamic publishing enterprise, and launched the Institute's own radio station, one of the first in the USA. Dr James Gray, President of the Institute from 1904 to 1934, often declared, 'It was the brains and heart of H. P. Crowell that brought this institution up, that made this Institute.'

Diversification

Henry's vision and leadership qualities were also key factors in the phenomenal growth of the Quaker Oats company. By 1906 it was strong enough to acquire all the assets of American Cereal and be incorporated as an operating company.

Building on the success of his famous breakfast cereal, Henry began to diversify. By 1907 Quaker Oats was the world's largest producer of animal feeds. In addition, more than two million barrels of white flour were produced annually. Energetic marketing abroad was also bringing huge rewards and by 1908 the company could proudly proclaim that the Quaker Oats trademark 'is known by more people in more countries than any other brand on any kind of goods in the world'.

Battle with the Chicago underworld

With so much to occupy him, Henry remarkably found time to become involved in the fight against vice in Chicago. In 1907 the city had been rocked by alarming revelations of an organized sex trade involving a network of some of its most influential citizens, including politicians, lawyers and the police. With so many powerful people involved, the authorities had been unable to stop the trade.

Henry was horrified and wanted to do something to protect vulnerable young women from exploitation. With four like-minded friends he formed the Committee of Five to spur the authorities to make investigations and prosecutions. It was brave to take on the Chicago underworld but the mood of the city was behind them and they began to make a difference. Soon they became the Committee of Fifteen and achieved some spectacular successes. They helped get the red light district with its five hundred brothels closed down and a Federal act passed to prevent traffic in women.

Of course, vice would always exist in Chicago. At one stage the group was up against no less a foe than the city's most notorious gangster, Al Capone, a ruthless killer who ran prostitution, gambling and bootlegging rackets. Nevertheless, however dangerous the opposition, Henry was undeterred and remained active in the group for the rest of his life.

Concern for Susan's health

It was thanks to his robust constitution that Henry was able to do so much in so many spheres, but Susan was less fortunate with her health. By 1909 it had become clear that she needed to spend the winter months in a friendlier climate. After much prayer, she and Henry decided to buy a property called Green Court just outside Augusta in Georgia.

They instantly felt at home in Green Court and started Bible classes there for the local community. Their influence was profound, almost every church in Augusta acknowledging that these Bible studies were a source of spiritual enrichment for many.

The Wyoming Hereford Ranch

At the age of sixty-six, when others might be easing back in their business activities, Henry spearheaded yet another successful enterprise. He had loaned money to a friend to buy a 55,000-acre ranch near Cheyenne in Wyoming and set up a cattle business but when the business failed in 1921, Henry took it over.

He stocked the ranch with 1,000 Hereford cows and 50 Hereford bulls as well as 2,500 cattle of other breeds. With the help of a first-class manager he so improved the quality of the Hereford breed that his cows won award after award. Henry himself was publicly honoured for 'his contribution toward agriculture in the development of the Hereford industry'. The ranch eventually earned international recognition.

Susan dies

Just a year after Henry had taken on the Hereford ranch, Susan's health steadily declined. She had been suffering with a heart problem and one day in June 1922, just after Henry had left Winnetka for a business trip, she took an unexpected turn for the worse. She sent a telegram urging him to come home. He raced back, desperately worried. When he arrived he sat by her bedside and they talked together, fondly recalling special times in their thirty-four years of marriage. These were precious moments but there would not be many more. Susan continued to deteriorate and sadly, on 17 June 1922, she died.

For the second time in his life Henry had to suffer the heartache of losing a dearly loved wife. Although the assurance that she was in God's safe keeping was clearly a great comfort to him—'She went to be with her Lord. She was a beautiful Christian character'—the loneliness he felt without her was unbearable.

Active into old age

Once again, as after Lillie's death, Henry threw himself into his work.

There was plenty to keep him busy. He had three businesses to oversee, a responsible position with the Moody Bible Institute and an ongoing battle with the Chicago underworld. He maintained his involvement in all these activities well into old age.

At the age of eighty-seven, although officially retired as Chairman of the Board of Quaker Oats, he continued to serve the company as honorary chairman and worked regular office hours. His daily routine remained unchanged, commuting from Winnetka to Chicago and walking the seven blocks from the station to his office in the Board of Trade Building where the company was based. On Tuesdays he walked from his office to the Moody Bible Institute to preside at the Executive Committee meetings.

He was also enthusiastically engaged in Christian outreach work. In 1943, aged eighty-eight, he wrote to a friend:

> I am glad to report that I am keeping well and able to carry on in all branches of life much to the surprise of many, who think that I should take less interest in the activities and efforts that are being put forth for making the Lord Jesus Christ known to men. The Lord is evidently preserving this body of mine . . . to be active.

Chicago says goodbye to Henry

Monday, 23 October 1944 seemed like any other day, with Henry following his normal routine. However, as he was leaving his office after work some of his employees noticed how pale he looked. Being a little late, he rushed to the station and arrived just in time to catch the train. Out of breath, he stepped on board, found a seat and, as usual, took out his New Testament to read on the journey. But he did not reach Winnetka. As the train began to pull out of the station it suddenly jerked to a halt. A passenger had alerted the guard that Henry was dead.

News of Henry's death met with great sadness in Chicago. His funeral took place three days later at the Moody Bible Institute where his body lay in state. His right hand was resting on his heart and holding the New Testament he always carried with him. Countless mourners from all walks of life filed past his coffin to pay their last respects, many in tears.

In his address, Dr William Houghton, President of the Moody Bible Institute, told the congregation: 'Henry P. Crowell was the most Christlike man I have ever met, bearing to the full that distinctive mark of the

Christian—humility. . . . But what makes possible such a character as Mr Crowell? The answer is clear and unmistakable. If you could ask him, his answer would humbly be in one word—Christ.'

After the service Henry's body was conveyed to Lake View Cemetery in Cleveland where he was laid to rest with Lillie and Susan.

Fitting memorials

On 5 February 1945 a new twelve-storey administration building was unveiled at the Moody Bible Institute. Henry had laid the foundation stone in 1938 but had declined Dr Houghton's request at the time to name it Crowell Hall in his honour, quietly explaining: 'Years ago I told the Lord that if He would allow me to make money for His service, I would keep my name out of it so He could have the glory.' After Henry's death Dr Houghton felt it was now acceptable to name the building Crowell Hall in Henry's memory and in recognition of all he had done for the Institute.

It was a fitting memorial to a great man but Henry would have considered something far more important as his legacy. His greatest joy had been 'close union and fellowship with my Saviour who loves me and gave Himself for my salvation and that of all who come to Him by faith'. To know that he had helped others to find the same joy by introducing them to Jesus Christ would have been memorial enough for him.

WILLIAM HARTLEY,
'the greatest name in jam-making'

'We have great competition and the house that makes the best article at the most reasonable price should win. I want us to be that house.' When William Hartley said those words he meant them. During his lifetime he established Hartley's as the leading brand of jam in the UK, a position it still proudly holds today. Hartley's products are also sold across the world.

In achieving his phenomenal success William Hartley was not driven by selfish ambition. The purpose of his life, he said, was to 'serve the Lord every day to the best of my ability'. His greatest joy was using his immense wealth to enrich the lives of others.

Growing up in Colne

William Pickles Hartley (Pickles was his mother's maiden name) was born in Colne, Lancashire, on the edge of the Pennines. It was principally a cotton-weaving town when William was born there on 23 February 1846. His father, John, was a tinsmith and a local Methodist preacher. His mother, Margaret, ran a small grocery shop in Colne. Sadly, William was the only one of their children to survive infancy.

He was immensely grateful for his Christian upbringing and stated: 'My parents and grandparents were godly people. I was always under the deepest religious impressions.' He also gratefully acknowledged the influence of his chapel Sunday school teacher whose character and deep spirituality made a lasting impression on him. As a result of these influences William declared: 'I never remember a time when I had not an earnest desire to be good.'

The Hartley family were members of the Primitive Methodist Church, a branch of Methodism that aimed to be as close as possible to the denomination's earliest roots, thus 'primitive' meaning 'original'. William became a full member of his local chapel at thirteen, the youngest permissible age. Around the same time he learned to play the harmonium used in the chapel's services. He very quickly mastered the instrument and became the chapel's official organist, holding this position for many years. In addition to playing at every service, he was responsible for training the choir. In due course he also became a Sunday school teacher and the chapel's treasurer.

It was quite normal at the time William was growing up for children as young as eight to work six and a half hours a day, six days a week in the cotton mills. However, John and Margaret denied themselves the extra income William could have brought into the home had they sent him out to work. Instead, they enrolled him at a local school founded by a voluntary organization for the education of working-class children. At thirteen he transferred to Colne Grammar School.

First steps in business

On leaving the grammar school at fourteen, William hoped to become a chemist but as there were no opportunities in Colne he worked in his mother's grocery shop. It was here that he discovered an appetite for commerce. After two years in the shop he became frustrated that the business could not grow in its small, cramped premises. When he heard that a much larger shop was available in Colne's main street he tried to persuade Margaret to take it and allow him to run it. She flatly refused, dismissing his idea as 'headstrong rashness'. It worried her that her son was capable of such foolish thinking.

However, a fellow chapel member whose opinion Margaret respected managed to convince her that William's idea was actually very sensible. In the end she bought the shop and put William in charge of it. And so, at sixteen, he became a businessman. And it quickly became obvious that he was a very good one.

At a time when there was no proper refrigeration he saw the need for a saltery, somewhere for people to buy ready salted food or have their own food salted to prolong its life. He therefore added this facility to his grocery business. He also saw further opportunity for growth by offering local retailers a wholesale service, selling them grocery items in bulk.

In developing the wholesale side of his business, William walked long distances across the moors to collect orders or make deliveries and often had to set off from home at five in the morning to get to his first customer by seven. Years later he recalled how tough it was: 'I walked to Haworth, Oakworth and to Keighley Station, so tired that I was very glad to sit down in the Station. I walked about twenty miles, I had called on twenty customers, and on many a journey I did not make a shilling. It took a good deal of resolution to keep that up.'

His 'resolution to keep that up' combined with his customers' trust in the reliability of his products won him an ever-growing clientele. He never mixed dubious ingredients into his items unlike some of his unscrupulous competitors after an easy profit. There was no brick dust in his cocoa or ground rice in his sugar. And his weights and measures were always accurate. Dishonest practice had been commonplace until the passing of the Adulteration of Food, Drink and Drugs Act in 1872 and against this background William's integrity stood out. As a result his business flourished.

Marriage

In May 1866, with the security of his thriving business behind him, William, aged twenty, married Martha Horsfield, his childhood sweetheart, now twenty-three. Martha was the daughter of a Colne grocer and the youngest of thirteen children, a sharp contrast to William who had grown up as an only child.

Their honeymoon was quite extraordinary seen through today's eyes. William gives us an account:

> We were married on a Whit-Monday morning. . . . Holidays were then a very rare thing in our native town of Colne. Indeed, we scarcely knew what the word 'holiday' was in the language. However, we were quite as happy with half a day on that Whit-Monday as we have been since with a month's holiday. On that afternoon we spent our honeymoon in processioning [through] the town of Colne with the Sunday School scholars and singing the special Whitsuntide hymns in the principal streets of our native town; and I was at business as usual next morning as though nothing had happened.

Their marriage was to be a long and happy one. They were to have eight daughters and a son. Martha proved to be the perfect wife for William. Like him, she had a deep Christian faith and she supported him wholeheartedly in all his church and philanthropic activities. She had a sharp mind and an instant grasp of business. She became a familiar figure at his works and frequently gave him wise and welcome advice in business matters.

The jam manufacturer is born

By the time he was twenty-five, William's business had grown to become one of the largest wholesale operations in Lancashire. Despite the demands on his time, he never allowed his church activities to suffer. As he explained:

> In those early days I paid the closest attention to my business, but on Sundays I always devoted the whole day to work in connexion with the chapel. . . . [M]y Sunday duty was: Sunday School 9 o'clock, service at 10.30, school at 1.15, afternoon service at 2.30, evening service at 6, prayer meeting at 7.30, and occasionally an open-air mission at 5.30 previous to the evening service.

But in an unexpected twist of circumstances, the nature and direction of his business changed. His jam supplier had become unreliable so William stopped doing business with him. But this left him in a difficult position: there was no other source of supply. Not wanting to disappoint his customers, he made a life-changing decision: he would make jam himself. And so, in the summer of 1871, with a workforce of twelve, he produced his first hundred tons.

From the outset he was determined that only the best quality would do. As with the contents of other products he sold, his jam would contain no dubious ingredients. There would be no turnips to boost the weight, no carrots as a substitute for sugar, no tiny chips of wood to look like seeds. He scrutinized the entire manufacturing process to ensure the purity and cleanliness of his product.

William's jam was an instant success and the price was reasonable. Sales went from strength to strength. Within three years the demand so greatly exceeded supply that he decided to give up the wholesale business and concentrate solely on jam-making. But was Colne the right place to do this?

Relocation to Bootle

There were compelling reasons to stay in Colne. He loved his home town, his business was thriving, he had a settled family life with Martha and his four daughters and he was happy in his chapel. But it made no sense to build a larger factory there. He needed to be more strategically placed on the railway network for distribution purposes, nearer to the Liverpool sugar refineries to reduce transportation costs of sugar to his works, nearer to the Mersey docks to reduce transportation costs to his works of oranges for marmalade production and close to fruit-growing farms. After weighing up all the options, he found that Bootle ticked all these boxes. He felt strongly that he should relocate there.

He told family and friends what he had in mind but was wholly unprepared for their reaction. 'There was no exception to the adverse criticism,' he said. Everyone accused him of 'vaulting ambition'. Why wasn't he satisfied with what he had? They warned him that he was tempting fate by being so greedy and predicted disaster.

Their comments hurt him very deeply. He wrote later that he 'never felt so alone'. But despite total lack of support, he was convinced he had to go. And so he sold his wholesale business in Colne and in June 1874 opened a factory in Pine Grove, Bootle, next to the Leeds–Liverpool Canal.

Early struggles in Bootle
William and Martha left Colne with their four daughters and moved into 12 Park Street close to the factory. Things soon started to go wrong. Within a year they tragically lost their youngest daughter, also called Martha, aged just nineteen months. And in the business sphere there were crushing pressures.

William had invested all his available capital in the construction of the new works and needed a loan to buy fruit and sugar. But it was difficult to find a lender. The first offer he received was on the condition that the lender be made a partner but Martha persuaded William against this. The only loan he could get was over seven years at an exorbitant rate which swallowed 75 per cent of his profits. As a result, money was extremely tight, both at home and in the business. William was continually burdened by financial worries and worked long hours to try to make ends meet. 'For a number of years in our early days we had great difficulties and our first struggles were severe indeed,' he recalled.

The joy of giving
The pressures on William in no way deflected him from his commitment to the Bootle Primitive Methodist Chapel where the family worshipped.

Chapter 4

He served faithfully as the organist, playing at every service and spending considerable time training the choir.

In the midst of their severe financial difficulties William and Martha made an incredible decision that seemed to defy all logic. It was a decision that revealed the depth of their Christian faith. William tells the story:

> Probably the greatest event of my life occurred on January 1, 1877. On that day my wife and I made a written vow that we would devote a definite and well-considered share of our income for religious and humanitarian work, and that this should be a first charge, and that we should not give to the Lord something when we had finished with everything else.

They decided, whatever their personal needs, to give 10 per cent of their gross income to 'the needs of mankind'. What moved them to do this? As William once wrote to a friend: 'When we think of the life and sacrifice of Jesus Christ, then nothing we can do is too much.'

The realization that he could use money to make a significant difference to the lives of others was a liberating experience for William. He said that it marked the beginning of 'the real, deep, lasting, and genuine happiness of my own Christian life'. He and Martha resolved that the percentage they would give should increase in proportion to the growth of their income, and even if their circumstances took a dramatic downturn, they would never give less than 10 per cent. In fact, their giving over the years continually increased, eventually reaching 30 per cent of gross income.

William asked God to show him where the money should be placed. He did not want to give randomly or impulsively: 'My daily prayer is that God will show me what He wishes me to do. I only want to see clearly His guiding hand, and I am daily asking Him to lead me.'

He admitted it was not easy at first to carry out this resolve. He was shocked to find that his natural instinct as an entrepreneur was to make money, not give it away. He described his inner conflict in the following way: 'The lower self at once asserted its claim, and said, "I have it, and it is mine." But the higher self, if it was in full sympathy with the teaching of Jesus Christ, would rise above the temptation and be ready in some reasonable degree to share with others.' As he began to form the habit of giving, William became aware that his selfish impulses gradually weakened. Eventually he was able to say: 'The more we cultivate the spirit of Jesus Christ, the easier the thing becomes, and what appeared to us quite impossible at the beginning becomes not only possible but absolutely a joy.'

During his times of struggle William never lost sight of his obligation to his customers. He maintained the highest standards of production and kept his prices at very reasonable levels. He declared: 'Our aim has always been to win the confidence of the public by making the best possible article and selling it at a fair price, and on that principle our business has gone from strength to strength.'

Such was the reputation of Hartley's jam that demand soared and an extension to the factory had to be built. Then another. The growth of the business was unstoppable. Despite the punitive nature of the loan, William was in a position to repay the outstanding balance well before the seven years of the loan were up. But the lender refused. The interest payments were much too attractive.

Challenge offers

As he had vowed, William unhesitatingly shared his good fortune with others. He frequently donated enormous sums of money unconditionally but sometimes, to discourage an over-reliance on handouts, he adopted the principle of 'challenge offers'. He wanted people to experience, as he had done, 'the luxury of doing good'. He would donate a specified amount towards a stated target on condition that the balance was found by the collective efforts of others.

When he learned in 1884 that the Primitive Methodist Missionary Society was in deep financial trouble, he immediately offered to help. The Society had accumulated a debt of £5,000—a massive amount at the time—and did not have the resources to pay it. In accordance with his principle of challenge offers William offered to pay £1,000 of the Society's debt if the balance of £4,000 could be raised. This had exactly the effect he wanted. It appealed to people's imagination and they rose to the challenge. Within a year £4,542 was raised and the debt cleared. William eventually became treasurer of the Missionary Society and regularly gave it generous financial support.

Relocation to Aintree

In 1885, after eleven years of continual growth, William's business was incorporated as William Hartley & Sons Ltd. By this time no further growth in Bootle was possible as all available space for extension had been exhausted. Once again William decided to relocate.

But this time he was not tormented by accusations of 'vaulting ambition' and gloomy predictions of disaster. Remembering the pain these had caused him—and reflecting on the success he had achieved in Bootle—he urged caution on those who were too easily prepared to pass judgement. Without intending in the slightest to be triumphalist (William never bore grudges), he openly stated: 'Whenever I look back upon that stirring period of my life, I often think how careful we should be in forming adverse views as to the conduct of others for fear that our criticism should prove to be wrong. It was so in my case.'

He found an ideal site for a new works at the junction of two major railway lines and within easy reach of the Liverpool docks. It was in open countryside about three miles to the east of Bootle close to the village of Aintree, home of the famous Grand National steeplechase. Opening in 1886, the factory became one of the largest of its kind in the world, producing six hundred tons of jam a week, enough to fill 1.3 million one-pound earthenware pots. About a quarter of the world's Seville oranges were shipped here.

William had a permanent workforce of eight hundred which rose to two thousand in the busy summer season when the fruit was harvested. He could easily have employed a steady number of employees throughout the year but, unlike other jam manufacturers who pulped their fruit and added preservatives to maintain a constant monthly rate of production, he made his jam as soon as the fruit arrived in the factory. This led to the confident claim 'Fruit gathered at sunrise is Hartley's Jam the same evening'.

To maintain the quality and the distinctive taste of his jam, William personally sampled each boiling and inspected up to a thousand jars at a time. He wanted nothing but the best for his customers. In fact, the company's trademark was a lighthouse, a Christian symbol associated with trust and safety. He wanted his customers to know his products were trustworthy.

But maintaining standards was a constant challenge. For one thing, the unreliability of the weather caused many problems. Too little sunshine caused a slower rate of ripening which delayed the start of the production process. Late frost or too much rain led to a reduced crop, while too large a crop resulted in wastage because much of it would deteriorate faster than it could be processed. Suppliers were another problem. They were often unreliable, sometimes delivering fruit late or delivering fruit that was either too small, not fully ripe or over-ripe.

The stress of these problems, combined with the day-to-day demands of running the company, often exhausted William. At times it affected his health and, despite his naturally cheerful temperament, sometimes made him depressed. He repeatedly ignored advice to slow down. He did, however, refuse to open a factory in the USA, despite good sales to that market. He knew he couldn't spread himself thinly enough to control quality both at home and in the States.

'My people'

Whatever the pressures on himself, William ensured they were not passed on to his workers. In the treatment of his employees, he said that he always tried 'to carry out the teaching of Jesus Christ'. He referred to them as 'my people' and knew each one by name. He enjoyed 'the happiest relations' with them.

Their working conditions mattered to him. The factory was well ventilated, and wholesome, well-prepared food was sold in the dining hall at cost price. If he noticed a task was physically too demanding, he would ask: 'What can be done to take the hardness out of this job? Never mind the cost.' When he discovered that he personally wasn't able to push a truck in a newly delivered batch, he ordered, 'Scrap them!'

As women outnumbered men by four to one, he looked for every possible means of making their work light and safe. He had all the tram lines in the factory laid out at very gentle gradients to make it easier for them to push loaded trucks. He also had sunken floor areas built for them to stand in so that they could fill pots with jam at a comfortable level with the work surfaces. This would save them having to bend.

He provided free medical care, employing the full-time services of a doctor and nurse. He also established a pension fund which he wholly financed himself. No contributions were ever asked from the workforce. The fund provided a means of income for any employee who had reached retirement age or could no longer work because of accident or illness. One year he took every employee over the age of eighteen on a five-day visit to Scotland. He paid not only all hotel and travel costs but also everyone's full wages for the duration of the trip.

Hartley's Village

In 1888, two years after the factory had opened, William built a garden village alongside it to create a pleasant and healthy living environment for his employees. It became known as Hartley's Village. It had an ornamental lake and a bowling green, and close by was a sports field. The streets were tree-lined and named after ingredients used in jam-making, such as Sugar Street, Spice Street and Plum Street. Each house had a front garden and running water, a luxury at the time. In spite of the superior quality of these homes, William deliberately kept the rents 'exceedingly low' as he did not want to make a profit from them.

Shortly afterwards he built a Primitive Methodist Church nearby for his employees. He and his family worshipped there themselves when they later moved close to the factory. Two of his daughters were married there.

Profit-sharing

William believed he had a moral obligation to share his wealth with those who helped create it. He considered his employees equal partners in a shared enterprise and told them: 'Our interests are mutual. I cannot carry on the business without your co-operation and I venture to think that in my capacity as your employer I render some service to you.'

In 1889 he introduced an annual profit-sharing scheme. He distributed the profits according to individual performance and spent long periods familiarizing himself with each person's work. He stressed he was not there to judge but to encourage: 'I must be in personal touch with practically every one of my workpeople and I am sure it works well. They all feel that they are not lost in the size of the business but are in direct contact with me, and they like this. . . . There is nothing like it for cementing good feeling between employer and employed.'

Other manufacturers were intrigued by the scheme, assuming there must be some commercial benefit in it. They wanted to know more. William explained to them: 'Profit-sharing is over and above a fair and just wage, and is given, not because I think it pays commercially . . . but because it seems to me right, and doing as I would be done by.' The enquirers immediately lost interest.

The annual distribution of profits was a special social occasion with music. It was as happy for William as it was for his employees. He told them: 'Whatever pleasure it gives you to receive the profit-sharing, I can say with perfect sincerity that it gives me equal pleasure to hand it to you.'

'Doing as I would be done by'

There were other ways in which William put into practice the principle of 'doing as I would be done by'. One was to ensure that his employees always received a fair wage. He publicly declared that if anyone in any department of the works could show that they were paid less than the workers in rival companies, he would increase their wages immediately. In fact, his wages were already higher than those of his competitors. From time to time he actually increased the wages of all his employees without being asked. No one ever complained about their earnings.

William would sometimes show his appreciation for good work in the most unexpected way. On one occasion, when a boiler had been built in record time, he asked the man concerned to come and see him. On the table in William's office were several piles of gold coins, each pile worth £50 (about £6,000 today). When the man came in, William placed one of the piles in an envelope, handed it over to him and quietly left before the man could thank him. He encouraged any employee in financial trouble to come to him for help and established a Benevolent Fund for this purpose. He was always very sympathetic in cases of genuine distress but he made it clear that debts incurred as a result of drink or gambling would meet with no sympathy.

A black hole

While ever looking for ways to improve the welfare of his workers, William also kept a watchful eye on the well-being of the Primitive Methodist Church. At a time when it found itself in a deep financial crisis he came to its help with an imaginative idea. During a period of national prosperity the Primitive Methodists had embarked on an ambitious chapel and school-building programme. No one could have foreseen that the programme would be brought to an abrupt end by a depression that unexpectedly hit the country. The only way of meeting the high construction costs was with the help of loans. And they were very expensive.

Aware of a spirit of panic, William urged calm. To avoid loans with exorbitant interest rates he proposed that the denomination should create an investment company of its own to lend money at reasonable rates and with easy repayment terms. His idea was dismissed as impractical.

But as the crisis deepened and no better solution was found, his idea began to gain acceptance. The result was the registration of the Primitive Methodist Chapel Aid Association Limited in 1890 with himself as treasurer.

There was, of course, one obvious requirement to make the Association work—investors. Without them there would be no money to lend. Not surprisingly, an untried company offering low interest rates was hardly an attractive proposition and investors were reluctant to come forward.

William acted quickly to create confidence. He publicly declared that he would invest his own money in the Association even though he could get much better returns elsewhere. He placed a huge amount into the Association's funds, immediately providing capital for loans. Others followed his lead and in a short time investments far exceeded expectations. With money now available to borrow on very favourable terms, the Primitive Methodist Church gradually cleared its debts and was able to climb out of a very black hole.

The split at Everton Football Club

William's keen social conscience and willingness to help others involved him in many public causes. One to which he was deeply committed was temperance, the fight against alcohol and the misery it caused. He supported a number of local organizations dedicated to this aim and was active nationally as Vice-president of the British Temperance League. He was also a staunch member of the Liberal Party which supported the temperance cause. Through these channels he came to know members of the management committee of Everton Football Club in Liverpool. When a serious crisis arose at the club in 1891 he became involved in it.

The trigger was a clash with Everton's president, John Houlding, over financial matters. Houlding owned the club's ground in the Anfield district and when he wanted to increase the rent for its use there was fierce opposition. There was also fierce opposition to his proposal that the club should buy his ground and be incorporated as a company. The committee considered his asking price to be exorbitant.

But opposition to Houlding operated at a much deeper level. He was a brewer and one of his public houses, The Sandon, was Everton's HQ. This was wholly incompatible with the strong temperance climate within the club and it extended into the political sphere. Houlding was a prominent member of the Conservative Party which looked after the interests of brewers. Most members of the Everton management committee, on the other hand, were active members of the temperance-supporting Liberal Party. William, as a Liberal councillor on Liverpool City Council, was well aware of the tension this caused within the club.

The serious clash of values with his committee finally led Houlding to expel them from Anfield in 1892 and continue Everton Football Club there without them. But one of his most outspoken opponents on the committee, George Mahon, appealed to the Football Association (the game's ruling body) claiming that Houlding had no legal right to the name 'Everton'. The appeal was upheld. Houlding was informed he could continue to run a club at Anfield but it must be under a different name. He chose Liverpool Association Football Club. A famous local rivalry was born.

Anticipating expulsion from Anfield, Mahon had already found a site on which to construct a new stadium about a mile away across Stanley Park. But there was a serious shortfall of capital. If it was not found the stadium could not be built, and without a ground the club would lose its place in the Football League and probably go out of existence.

William and a number of others came to the rescue, forming a consortium pledged to supply the crucial shortfall as an interest-free loan without expectation of return if things went wrong. There were loud cheers when his was the first of the sponsors' names to be read out at a large public gathering. He was one of two people who pledged the largest single amount. The new stadium, named Goodison Park after the road in which it stood, was opened on 24 August 1892 amidst great fanfare. The club's continued existence and its place in the Football League were now secured. For his part in making this possible, William is still heralded today as one of the saviours of Everton Football Club.

Chapter 4

Aintree Institute and the Beatles

It was William's commitment to the temperance cause that drew him into the dispute at Everton. His commitment to this cause was evident in other ways, too. Determined to do what he could to provide a counter-attraction to drink, he conceived the idea of a well-equipped community and recreation centre to be built near his works. He had in mind a building with a concert hall accommodating 650 people, a gymnasium, billiards rooms, classrooms, a lecture room and dining rooms. It would be surrounded by bowling greens and tennis courts. He wanted this centre to be much more than a private initiative. He was keen to foster a spirit of cooperation in humanitarian work between churches across denominational divides. His dream was of a centre 'for everything that was elevating and of a Christlike character' run by an interdenominational committee. He put the idea to a meeting of church representatives in March 1892 and offered £1,000 (£125,000 today) to get the project going.

But the idea was rejected. For another two and a half years he tried to win support for it but met with no enthusiasm. He finally admitted that if the centre was to be built, he would have to fund it alone. Disappointed but undeterred, he saw the project through. The Aintree Institute was opened on 3 November 1896.

It ran successfully as a recreation centre for well over a century. It has a close association with the Beatles. Prior to the release of their first record, they played there fifty-two times.

Queen Victoria's Diamond Jubilee

Another cause close to William's heart was the fight against sickness and disease. He gave vast amounts of money for the construction of hospitals, for the endowment of beds and for medical research. He financed cancer research at Liverpool University and also supported the university's School of Tropical Medicine, not least because of its benefits for missionary work. His generous giving extended far and wide but he never forgot the needs of his home town, Colne.

Although he had left Colne for business reasons, his affection for the town remained deep and lasting. He kept up to date with its affairs by subscribing to the local newspaper and it thrilled him to meet old friends there: 'It's like meat and drink to me to see those people.'

Reading the Colne newspaper one day in 1897, he noticed a report of a meeting considering how to commemorate Queen Victoria's Diamond Jubilee. He immediately wrote to the Mayor with a proposal: 'I am willing to provide the money to build and furnish a Cottage Hospital for Colne.' But he made a condition intended to stimulate others to give, too: 'that the people of Colne and neighbourhood subscribe a similar amount for an endowment fund'. In other words, he would build the hospital but—at a time when there was no National Health Service—the public must be willing to pay for its running.

William's condition was accepted and planning went ahead. At the Mayor's invitation, he laid the foundation stone of the hospital on 1 April 1899. In his address, William referred to the responsibility of wealthy people such as himself to help others: 'The teaching of Jesus Christ was that those who . . . turned up at the top, owed a great debt, and by a portion of their money, knowledge and time, they should redeem this debt for the benefit of those who were less endowed.'

The building was completed within twelve months and opened on 20 April 1900.

Pleas for help

As a public benefactor known for his generosity, William received countless pleas for help. He gave each one personal and prayerful consideration, knowing he needed to exercise wisdom and sensitivity in the distribution of 'the Lord's money', as he called it. He considered himself merely the steward, not the owner, of the money he made.

He was always conscious that financial help given to one might easily be at the expense of another deserving case of need. Of course, the careful examination of requests for help was a time- consuming process but William considered it necessary if he was to make the right decisions. He also felt that merely giving money was not, in itself, enough. He believed he should also become actively involved with causes he financed by attending relevant meetings and events. Again, this made great demands on his time but he gave it willingly.

He also gave anonymously and had a network of trusted friends whose task it was to inform him of cases of dire need. He never questioned his friends' judgement; he only ever asked if the amount they recommended was actually enough.

New factory in London

William's generosity was accompanied by the continual growth of his business. Sales of his jam had been booming in the North and Midlands but gradually southerners who had holidayed in the North had become aware of it and began to look for it back home. Furthermore, established customers moving south were keen to continue buying it. Demand in the South became so great that William decided to start production in London with the help of his son John.

He found a suitable site in Green Walk, Bermondsey, and built a new factory on it. When finished, it was one of the capital's largest. It was formally opened on 25 June 1901. At the opening ceremony William proudly told reporters: 'The supreme object will be to turn out the purest and best article which the most advanced science and art of preserve-making can command. Hartley's makes only one quality—the best.'

It was a claim he lived up to. He took the greatest care in the selection of fruit and ensured it was cleaned with specialist machines on arrival at the factory. Three doctors who inspected the manufacturing process gave the following glowing report: 'We are exceedingly well pleased with the entire arrangements. The fruit was most excellent; its condition could not have been better, and everything used in the manufacture of the jam was all that we could desire.'

As the reputation of Hartley's jam continued to spread in the South, the works had to be enlarged twice to keep up with demand. Such was the volume of business that there was a constant shuttle of deliveries along Tower Bridge Road between the factory and its own private wharf on the Thames.

Incredibly, William made little use of advertising in achieving his success. When a new salesman wrote to him asking for a sample of the company's products to display, William confidently replied: 'Dear Sir, The name is the sample.' This was not arrogance. It was an accepted fact that Hartley's did indeed make 'the best'.

Supporting medical research

In 1901, the same year that his London factory was opened, William saw work commence on new botanical laboratories he had funded at Liverpool University. The Botany Department had previously been housed in inadequate accommodation in old buildings. William valued the department's research into the medicinal properties of plants and was delighted to provide fully equipped laboratories in a purpose-built centre to facilitate work of such importance.

The centre was opened on 10 May 1902 and named the Hartley Botanical Institute in his honour. In an expression of gratitude to William at the ceremony, he was thanked not only for his generosity in funding the Institute but also 'for the personal interest he has shown in the details of its arrangement and equipment'.

In reply William explained how uplifting it was to be involved with organizations like the Botanical Institute. He told the audience that he found it liberating, as a businessman, to have 'an outlet from the commercial into the distinctively Christian atmosphere'.

He expanded this point on a later occasion when presenting workshops for the blind in Liverpool: 'A successful businessman needed some corrective, some safety valve, some definite means of escape into the larger life of the higher world.' At the same time he stressed that generosity is not measured by what people give but by what they have left. He had a very keen sense of perspective.

Hartley College, Manchester

Another of William's interests was education. He was a member of the Walton School Board during his time as a Liverpool councillor and made regular contributions towards the cost of lessons about the dangers of alcohol. He was also a major benefactor of the Primitive Methodists' theological college in Manchester where the denomination's ministers were trained. William twice funded major extensions to it, making it one of the largest theological colleges in Britain.

As Vice-president of the British and Foreign Bible Society William attached great importance to the teachings of the Bible. He wanted Primitive Methodist ministers to be so thoroughly grounded in biblical knowledge and understanding that they could provide quality teaching for their congregations. He felt that the current training period of two years was too short to ensure the proper standard was reached and tried to persuade the college authorities to extend it to three. Aware that such a move would involve an increase in student numbers and additional pressures on residential accommodation, he offered to provide the necessary funding.

At first there was no general agreement that extended training was necessary and so plans for development did not go ahead. Eventually, however, the wisdom of William's recommendation was realized and his offer of financial support accepted. Building work went ahead.

Within a few years the demand for Primitive Methodist ministers had grown to such an extent that a further extension was necessary. Once again, William provided the funding. This made possible the building of new staff and student accommodation, improved lecture facilities, a new library and a college chapel. These facilities were opened on 18 June 1906 and, in gratitude to William, the college was renamed Hartley College.

A knighthood

William's generosity extended to many more organizations and institutions than those already mentioned. By 1908 he was recognized as one of the country's leading philanthropists and was knighted by King Edward VII on 21 July that year 'in recognition of the many princely acts of beneficence and philanthropy rendered by Sir William to his country'. Colne was particularly proud of him—he was the first person from his home town to receive this honour.

Freedom of Colne

A year after receiving his knighthood, William was also honoured in his home town. At a meeting on 28 July 1909, the Mayor of Colne read out a resolution by the Town Council placing on record 'its appreciation of the high esteem in which Sir William Hartley of Aintree is held by the inhabitants of his native town; and in recognition of the many valuable services rendered by Sir William to the Borough, as well as to the community at large, that he should be created a Freeman of the Borough'. He went on to say: 'I am proud that we, in Colne, can claim such a gentleman as a native.'

At the Mayor's banquet at Colne town hall on 9 November William was formally presented with the award. In his reply he explained how much it meant to him:

The honour of being a Freeman of Colne touches me very much. . . . The ups and downs of life and the development of a business career often take men from the home of their childhood. That has been so in my case. But there are few men who do not retain happy memories of the playground of their youth and the place where their ambitions were born.

At the ceremony, appreciation was expressed to William for his gift of the cottage hospital and of the Hartley Homes, almshouses for the aged poor currently under construction. William responded by touching on a theme close to his heart:

I am very proud of my native town. If I am to judge from my own experience, the pleasure of memory is much enhanced when, after the lapse of years, one desires to share with his native town those fruits of prosperity which may be made helpful to the many who in the fulness of life are less happily circumstanced. It is . . . the first duty of those who have money to remember in a liberal manner those who have not. . . . Where much is given much is required.

Hartley Homes, Colne

The homes for the aged poor referred to above were opened two years later. They were built as a complex of twenty almshouses on a site with marvellous countryside views and surrounded by beautiful grounds. William not only paid for the houses to be built but also provided money for their upkeep and for the services of a gardener.

At the opening ceremony, he spoke fondly of his and Martha's association with Colne:

Lady Hartley and I are to-day on familiar ground. We were both born in Colne. We passed our early days here. We were both under the influence of good parents and teachers here, especially at Sunday School, whose wise counsel had a lasting effect upon us. Although we left Colne about thirty-eight years ago, we have never forgotten the helpful influences that surrounded us in our early days.'

At a time when women did not have the right to vote, he made a statement at the ceremony about the management of the homes that would have surprised, even shocked, many: 'My present idea is that one third of the management committee should be women. I dare say in a short time there will be ladies on the Colne Town Council. I could vote for that myself.' He was clearly a man ahead of his time.

Top honour in the Primitive Methodist Church

The same year he was awarded the Freedom of Colne William was elected unanimously to the highest position a layman could hold in the Primitive Methodist Church, President of the Conference. He was only the second non-ordained person within a hundred years to be entrusted with this important leadership role.

As president, he chaired meetings with great efficiency, ensuring that the delegates always kept to the point. On one occasion, when a matter of £20 was under debate, he remarked humorously, although pointedly, 'I could make the money in the time that you are talking about it.'

Financial problems were a regular cause of concern to the denomination and because of this many good projects could not go ahead. In one of his addresses, William was uncompromising in pointing out the solution: 'At present we are held back in our medical missions, our foreign missions, our home missions . . . for want of money. I am persuaded . . . that all our financial difficulties would soon disappear . . . if only every disciple of Jesus Christ willingly consecrated to the Master's service a definite share of his income.'

He explained why this wasn't happening: 'Primitive Methodists who are now successful men of business tell me . . . they cannot bring their mind to support religious and philanthropic enterprises with the liberality they should, not because they have not got the money, nor because they do not admit it to be their duty, but because they have not sufficiently developed the disposition to give.'

This was a message that William delivered on many occasions. He had the moral authority to do so because he led by example.

The *Titanic* disaster

In 1912 a tragedy occurred that shocked the world and plunged Colne into grief. In the early hours of 15 April, the world's largest liner, the *Titanic*, sank after hitting an iceberg on its maiden voyage across the Atlantic Ocean. Among the 1,517 dead was a native of Colne, thirty-three-year-old

Wallace Hartley. Although not related to Wallace, William, along with the people of Colne, felt a deep sense of personal loss. He was one of them.

Wallace, a devout Christian and an excellent violinist, was the leader of the eight-member band on the ship. As soon as he realized the *Titanic* was sinking, he assembled his musicians to play cheerful tunes on deck to calm and comfort the passengers. The band played continuously for two hours until the very end.

When the ship began to tilt for its final descent, Wallace thanked his fellow musicians and released them from duty. As they walked away, he struck up the opening notes of the hymn 'Nearer, My God, to Thee'. They turned back and joined him. Minutes later they were washed away and drowned.

The story of the band's bravery in the face of death inspired newspaper headlines worldwide. 'Nearer, My God, to Thee' became an anthem of courage and hope and symbolized light in the midst of darkness. It was played at the funerals and memorial services of many of those who had perished. Ten days after the sinking, Wallace's body—with his violin case strapped to it—was recovered by a search ship together with those of two of his band. He was the only one of the three brought back to England for burial. His funeral on 18 May became the focus of national grief and international attention.

It was held at the Bethel Methodist Church in Colne where he had been a choirboy. Designed to hold seven hundred people, about one thousand were present. Some forty thousand people—almost double the population of Colne—lined the streets as the cortège, led by several brass bands, made its way through the town. It took more than an hour to reach the cemetery a quarter of a mile away from the chapel.

On 24 May a memorial concert for the band took place at the Royal Albert Hall with seven of the world's leading orchestras combined into one, the largest ever assembled. It was conducted by some of the top conductors of the day including Sir Edward Elgar and Sir Henry Wood. The concert concluded with the singing of 'Nearer, My God, to Thee' with deep emotion by the whole audience.

Well before Wallace Hartley's funeral, Colne Town Council had decided to launch an appeal for funds to erect a memorial to him. William immediately made a challenge offer which was announced in *The Times*:

Chapter 4

'Sir W. P. Hartley, who is a native of Colne, has promised to contribute a sum equal to 10 per cent of the total amount subscribed towards the town's memorial to the bandmaster.'

The amount needed was duly raised. William's was the largest donation by a single individual.

First World War

Two years after the *Titanic* tragedy, an even greater catastrophe occupied the thoughts of the nation: the outbreak of the First World War. Almost immediately David Lloyd George, the Chancellor of the Exchequer, formed a small group of the best business minds in the country to advise him on crucial financial matters. William was one of them.

But not even the best business minds in the country escaped the devastating impact of the war. William felt its effects sharply. On the personal level he was overwhelmed with grief when his 'dearly loved grandson', Hartley Barkby, a nineteen-year-old officer with the Royal Field Artillery, was killed on the Somme in 1916.

On the business level things became so bad that at one point he wondered if his company would survive. Sugar was in short supply and its cost escalated. Fruit quantities were greatly reduced because increased acreage was allocated to the growth of essential crops such as wheat for bread. There was also a severe labour shortage due to enlistment in the armed forces.

Despite all this, the public noticed that Hartley's jam maintained its pre-war quality and prices were not raised. William was never tempted to take moral shortcuts, stating: 'We were resolved—I was very firm on it myself—not to make profit out of national necessities.'

However, no amount of external pressure could put a brake on his commitment to supporting worthy causes. He made generous donations to hospitals and to bodies such as the Red Cross and he gave financial support to the families of any of his employees serving in the armed forces. Martha personally delivered envelopes to them containing money.

Failing health

The strain of the war years took a great toll on William's health. By 1919 he was suffering angina attacks at the slightest exertion. That year he was offered the position of Mayor of Colne but declined on medical advice.

In view of his failing health, it was decided it would be sensible to move from his grand house on Lord Street, Southport, the family home of the previous fifteen years, to a more easily managed house in the Birkdale district of the town.

Fortunately, William's son-in-law, John Higham, eased his business pressures by helping to run the Aintree works. The London factory was already in his son John's hands. William was able, therefore, to devote more time to his philanthropic work.

New hospitals for Liverpool and Colne

Before the war, William had planned to fund two new hospitals, a maternity hospital in Liverpool and a larger, much better equipped hospital in Colne to replace the outdated cottage hospital. His original intention was to complete the Liverpool hospital in time for his Golden Wedding, but the outbreak of war put an abrupt end to his plans. He resolved, however, to resume the Liverpool and the Colne projects after the war.

By 1921 it was possible to pick up where he had left off. That year he donated a site for the Liverpool Maternity Hospital in Oxford Road and gave a huge sum of money towards the cost of building it. On 3 September he fulfilled his pre-war promise to Colne when he laid the foundation stone of a new hospital on a site directly next to the Hartley Homes he had built for the aged poor.

It is a measure of William's commitment to the fight against sickness and disease that he was undeterred by the phenomenal rise in post-war building costs. The new Colne hospital—to be named the Hartley Hospital—would now cost four times more to build than before the war. But he would cut no corners. In his address to the ten thousand people present when he laid the foundation stone, he declared: 'You can rely upon my promise that everything known to medical science will be provided in it and that nothing will be left undone to make it complete and up to date in every particular.' At the same time, he reaffirmed the close bond he and Martha felt with Colne: 'My wife and I never forget that we were born in Colne, and in the erection of this hospital we have endeavoured to show in a practical manner our affection for our native town.'

Death and funeral

William followed the building progress of the Hartley Hospital in Colne with close interest but sadly did not live to see it finished. In 1922, just a year after laying the foundation stone, his health problems caught up with him. When he went to bed on Tuesday, 24 October he told his daughter Christiana he felt unwell. Christiana, the only one of his seven daughters not married, was running the household. She checked on him three times in the night and was extremely worried that he seemed to be declining. When he woke in the morning he said he felt much better and intended to visit his works in Aintree. But he didn't get there. As he climbed out of bed he suffered a massive heart attack and died. He was seventy-six.

At the news of his death the flags at Southport Town Hall and Southport Liberal Club were flown at half-mast. His funeral service was held three days later at the Primitive Methodist Chapel in Derby Road, Southport, known locally as 'The Jam Chapel' because William had built it.

After the service William's body was transported by road some fifty miles to Colne for his burial in Trawden Cemetery in the hills above the town to be laid to rest with his parents and his little daughter Martha. The flag at Colne town hall was flown at half-mast and as the procession passed through the town to the cemetery all shops were closed and blinds drawn as a mark of respect for a great and much-loved man. Concurrent with the interment in the cemetery a service was held at the Aintree Primitive Methodist Chapel attended by many of William's grateful employees. His death had made national news and the following Sunday congregations in churches and chapels across the country paused respectfully to reflect on his life and passing.

The secret of William's success

William's products were widely regarded for their quality, even gracing the table of royalty. And when the renowned Polar explorer Robert Falcon Scott set out on his courageous Antarctic expedition of 1910–13 in an attempt to be the first man to reach the South Pole, he took supplies of Hartley's jam with him. After the First World War a former serviceman could write that Hartley 'gave the fighting Tommies his very best jams'. This was again the case during the Second World War, as the following company advertisement reveals: 'Hartley's give you their word that they will keep QUALITY UP and PRICES DOWN as long as is humanly possible' (their capitalization). The advertisement concluded with the slogan: 'HARTLEY'S—the greatest name in jam-making.' It was clearly a claim the company felt able to live up to.

Because Hartley's jam is still appreciated for its quality and taste, many would argue that the slogan remains valid today. No doubt it would have delighted William to know that the tradition he started of giving customers only the best lives on. But would he like to be remembered for this alone? Was this the sole secret of his success?

Today fame and fortune tend to define a person's worth and William would no doubt be admired for establishing a brand that made him enormously wealthy. But he would instantly have dismissed fame and fortune as the measure of a person's value or as a guarantee of happiness. He made this quite clear: 'Thank God, happiness is from within, not from without. It is what a man is, and not what a man has.' He was careful to apply the standard of 'what a man is' to himself: 'I am much exercised as to whether I am such a disciple of Jesus Christ that my work people, my business friends, my neighbours and my family can constantly see the Spirit of the Master in my actions.'

So what was the secret of success as William saw it? His own words provide a fitting conclusion to his story:

> My last word must be that we . . . followers of Jesus Christ, must carry into our life His spirit and teaching, and that whatever we think Jesus Christ would have done, had He been in our place, whether we are employers or employed, whether we are in business or out of business, *that* we are compelled to do. This is the secret of all true success: the consecration of ourselves and our substance to Him who loved us and laid down His life for us.

HENRY HEINZ
and his '57 Varieties'

'He showed . . . that the belief that business demanded ruthlessness and the cutting of moral corners was a superstition as foolish as it was evil. He built a business that proved it.'

Those words were written in 1923, four years after Henry Heinz's death, by his private secretary and biographer E. D. McCafferty. And Heinz proved beyond any doubt that it was possible to achieve brilliant business success without cutting moral corners. By the time of his death in 1919 he had established his company as the best-known brand name in the world and such was his standing that he could even count the President of the United States among his many admirers. It is an amazing success story and one that can be traced back to the simplest of beginnings when he was just eight years old.

Family background

Henry John Heinz was born in Pittsburgh, Pennsylvania, on 11 October 1844, the son of German immigrants. His father, John, came to the USA in 1840 at the age of twenty-nine and settled in Birmingham on Pittsburgh's south side where he worked as a brick-maker. His mother, Anna Schmidt, emigrated from Germany in 1843 at the age of twenty-one and also lived in Birmingham, meeting John and marrying him shortly after her arrival. They had eight children, four boys and four girls. Henry was their eldest.

Henry's parents had a profound influence on him and he, in turn, had the deepest respect for them. Looking back in later years, he wrote that he had 'an honest father' and a mother with 'a Christlike spirit'. He had a particularly close bond with his mother and it was to her that he attributed his Christian faith: 'In living for the Master and serving Him, some things have been incalculably helpful, and I turn . . . with grateful heart to the teachings of my mother.'

In fact, he considered his faith to be his mother's greatest legacy: 'to it I attribute any success I may have attained during my life'. He also acknowledged a great debt to the Sunday school he attended in developing his faith. Significantly, he never started any business project nor took any important personal decision in life without first making it a matter for prayer.

The spark is ignited

When Henry was five, the family moved to Sharpsburg, five miles northeast of Pittsburgh, where his father started his own brick-making business. He also bought a family home with a four-acre plot of land large enough for horse-grazing and the cultivation of vegetables. At the age of eight, Henry helped in the vegetable garden before and after school and hugely enjoyed it. The experience gave birth to a passion for food production that would eventually lead him into the world of business.

The garden produce far exceeded the Heinz family's needs. It was Henry's task, therefore, to make the rounds of local households with a basket of vegetables in each hand and sell as much of the surplus as he could. He took to the task like a duck to water. Such was his success that by the age of ten he had been given his own three-quarters of an acre to cultivate and a wheelbarrow to carry the produce.

His vegetable business flourished and by the age of twelve his allocation of land was increased to three and a half acres. From his profits he was able to buy a horse and cart. With these at his disposal he could sell to hotels and the central market in Pittsburgh eight miles away in addition to his regular household customers. His entrepreneurial instincts would not allow him to return from Pittsburgh with an empty cart. While at the market he bought other produce which he sold at a profit to grocers on the way home to Sharpsburg.

First great idea

As a young child Henry helped his mother to scrape and scrub horseradish roots until they were clean enough to be grated and preserved in salt and vinegar. Grated horseradish was a very popular accompaniment to beef and seafood but housewives found its preparation tedious and unpleasant.

It bruised their knuckles and made their eyes smart. By the time he was seventeen Henry realized he could save housewives a great deal of time and trouble by selling them good-quality bottled grated horseradish free of all impurities. Although bottled horseradish was already locally available, there was no telling what might be mixed with it. It could be turnips, soil, sand, sawdust or leaves; even insects found their way into it. Furthermore, these unwelcome ingredients could not be seen because unscrupulous sellers always used dark-coloured bottles to obscure the contents.

Henry refused to make quick profits by disregarding purity. He was determined to create a product that consumers could wholly trust and resolved to gain their confidence by using only clear, see-through bottles to make the contents transparent. From the very beginning he was determined never to compromise on quality and lived up to two mottoes he coined as guiding principles in all his business activities: 'To do a common thing uncommonly well brings success' and 'Quality is to a product what character is to a man'. He later met with hostility from unscrupulous manufacturers when he helped push through the Pure Food and Drug Act in the USA in 1906 which banned the manufacture, sale and transportation of adulterated and mislabelled food and drug products.

The superior quality of Henry's horseradish stood out from that of his competitors and found a ready market with housewives, grocers, hotels and butchers. In his first year of production sales grossed $2,400, an enormous amount at the time. Henry soon needed the help of two younger brothers and two of his sisters to meet the ever-growing demand.

Diversifying

In addition to his horseradish enterprise, Henry also became actively involved in his father's growing brick-making business. Following a course at Duff's Mercantile College in Pittsburgh, Henry became John's accountant and helped him in other ways too.

By the age of twenty-one Henry had made enough money from his sales of horseradish to buy a half-interest in his father's company which he felt had potential for even greater growth. He saw an opportunity for increased productivity when the plant closed down during the freezing winter months because brick-making was virtually impossible. Henry knew that if brick production could be kept going during the winter, the business would have a major advantage over its competitors. From his share of the profits he installed heating and drying equipment. This solved the problem. As a result he was able to meet an order for 750,000 bricks and also produce a substantial quantity of stock ready for sale in spring when demand was at its highest.

The continuing success of the business inspired Henry to start up a brick-making enterprise of his own while still keeping his father's accounts for him. In 1868, at the age of twenty-four, he bought a brickyard in Beaver Falls, Pennsylvania, and went into partnership with his close friend, L. C. (Clarence) Noble. It was agreed that Clarence would live in Beaver Falls and oversee operations at the plant while Henry would remain in Sharpsburg to spearhead sales. It was also agreed that Henry could continue his vegetable business alongside his sales activities for the brickyard.

Marriage to Sarah Young

A year later, on 23 September 1869, Henry married Sarah Sloan Young. She was always known as Sallie. Her parents were originally from County Down in the north of Ireland where her father had been a mill-owner. The family moved to Pittsburgh in the 1840s.

Their wedding venue was the First Methodist Protestant Church in Fifth Avenue, Pittsburgh. This was something of a compromise as Henry was a Lutheran and Sallie a United Presbyterian. The service was conducted by Rev. Ezra Morgan Wood who had achieved national fame for the eulogy he gave at President Lincoln's funeral. Henry and Sallie became members of the Fifth Avenue church and Henry served there as a Sunday School teacher, eventually becoming superintendent.

Henry and Sallie were to have five children, four sons and a daughter. Sadly, one of their sons lived only a month.

Launch of the Anchor brand

In the year of his marriage Henry decided to focus on food production as his sole business interest. That year he formed another partnership with Clarence—Heinz and Noble Company—to sell a range of food products under the brand name of Anchor. The image of an anchor on the company's products was significant. It had been a Christian symbol of hope since Roman times. By adopting it Henry was publicly associating the company with Christian values which included a guarantee of quality, honesty in business dealings and the resolve that all parties in a business transaction should benefit equally. Throughout his career he remained true to these values, publicly stating: 'The ruling principle of our business must be to secure the permanent satisfaction of the consumer and the full confidence of the trade.'

At first Henry and Clarence specialized in horseradish production, using Henry's Sharpsburg home as their centre of operations. Soon celery sauce and pickled cucumbers were added to their product range, making it necessary to rent an additional building.

Three years later Clarence's twenty-two-year-old brother, E. J. Noble, joined the expanding firm and it was renamed Heinz, Noble & Co. They extended their product range still further to include sauerkraut and vinegar but it was the sale of pickles (called pickled cucumbers in the UK) that accounted for the company's astronomical growth. Pickles were extremely popular, especially among the rapidly increasing number of German immigrants in the USA who firmly believed they had health-enhancing properties.

Sales of Heinz products began to boom. By 1875 the company was producing three thousand barrels of sauerkraut and fifteen thousand barrels of pickles annually. One hundred and sixty acres were under cultivation, mostly for cucumbers, but as markets continued to expand this acreage was inadequate and a further eight hundred acres were acquired on lease in Woodstock, Illinois. Furthermore, the increasing volume of produce made it impossible to operate from the old family house in Sharpsburg and so a four-storey factory and a warehouse were rented in downtown Pittsburgh. Expansion continued with the acquisition of a warehouse in Chicago and a factory in St Louis which in 1875 produced seventy-five thousand barrels of vinegar. There seemed to be no end to the Heinz success story.

What made it possible for the company to grow from a small, local operation to one that was beginning to make its mark nationally? The answer can be summed up in one word: quality. It was this that set it apart from its competitors and won the confidence of consumers who were always welcome to visit the factory in Pittsburgh to inspect the cleanliness of the manufacturing process and the purity of the products.

Chapter 5

The crash

The rapid growth of the company up to 1875 was even more remarkable when seen against the backdrop of a severe economic depression that hit the United States like a tidal wave in 1873. When the country's leading bank, Jay Cooke and Company, went bankrupt that year, it sparked off a panic. In a chain reaction other banks met the same fate in quick succession. Even the New York Stock Exchange closed for the first time in its history. Within two years some eighteen thousand businesses had failed and unemployment had rocketed. It took six years for the economy to stabilize again.

But the Heinz company's continuing success during the early depression years came under threat when very black clouds began to appear on the horizon. Investment in expansion had been high and in May 1875 cash-flow problems emerged. Henry's father had helped out with a loan but it was still a struggle to meet bills and pay wages. Remarkably, the Noble brothers did not appreciate the seriousness of the situation, believing it would pass, and carried on buying raw materials regardless. This added considerably to the growing financial pressure the business was under and led to a strain in the relationship between Henry and the Nobles.

A disastrous business decision made matters even worse. Henry had entered into an agreement with the company that owned the eight hundred acres in Woodstock to pay 60 cents a bushel for the entire cucumber crop, however large that might be. He was expecting a normal yield but was horrified when the crop that year proved to be a record. By the end of August cucumbers were being delivered to his salting stations at the rate of two thousand bushels and at a cost of $12,000 per day. Storage space ran out. Crates were squeezed into every available corner and soon the warehouse entrances were blocked. Overproduction was in every way a nightmare.

Where could Henry find the money to pay for this excessive crop as well as covering other substantial costs such as the wages of his 170 employees? The only way out of the crisis was to borrow but it was the middle of a recession and no one was lending. In fact, the banks started to call in the loans he already had and his cheques bounced. As his debts mounted creditors started to lean on him and the Nobles began to distance themselves from him. They did not want to be associated with the company's rapid downward slide. By early December the strain had seriously affected

Henry's health. For three days he was confined to bed suffering from painful boils.

There was no let-up. On 15 December the Pittsburgh factory was forced to close. Two days later Heinz, Noble & Co. filed papers in the US District Court for bankruptcy. The factory was emptied and its contents sold. But for Henry himself there was worse to follow. By order of the county sheriff, all his possessions were put up for sale; even Sallie's horse and buggy had to go.

All this hurt deeply but it was the attitude of friends, neighbours and even relatives that stung him most. The Noble brothers completely turned their backs on him. Clarence, his best friend after whom he had named his son, told everyone that Henry alone was responsible for the firm's collapse. Henry even had to defend himself against an unjust smear campaign accusing him of fraud. An acute sense of abandonment overwhelmed him, prompting him to write: 'I find few friends when we are known to have no cash and are bankrupt.' Things were so bad he even had to borrow money to buy food. Remarkably, in the midst of all his troubles, he somehow managed to honour his teaching commitments in the Sunday school although it was clearly an enormous struggle.

He hit his lowest point on Christmas Day. He was penniless and unable to give either Sallie, his six-year-old daughter Irene or his four-year-old son Clarence any presents. It was an intensely painful time for him and what made it even more unbearable was the fact he could see how upset Sallie was despite her brave efforts to hide it.

His mother's prayer

It was his mother who helped lift him out of the black cloud of depression. On Christmas Day she gave him a card on which she had composed a prayer. He was to treasure it for the rest of his life.

So great was the impact it made on him that he started a tradition in which a copy of the prayer, accompanied by a letter from himself, was passed down through the generations by Heinz fathers on Christmas Day. In the following extract from the letter, he explains what the prayer meant to him:

> This simple gift from my good mother, I hold as the greatest of my life.
> Coupled with its beautiful and comforting sentiment was the assurance

that 'the Lord will provide.' . . . It is hardly reasonable to expect this simple card and its tender sentiment to make the impression on your life that it has made on mine. If it could, it would be the means of keeping you humble, and of causing you to realize more and more as the years go by, your dependence upon the Giver of all good things.

A fresh start

Lifted and inspired by his mother's prayer Henry resolved to make a fresh start. His first priority was to compile a list of creditors. He entered the details of what he owed each one in a little book entitled 'M.O. BOOK OF HENRY J. HEINZ, 1875'. The 'M.O.' stood for Moral Obligations. Although he was not legally bound to repay his debts, he felt it was his Christian duty to do so.

He knew it would not be easy to start again. Regular customers had turned their backs on him, the Noble brothers had blackened his name and he had no money. His parents were suffering financial pressures after making great sacrifices to try to help him. His father even lost his brickyard. But the family continued to keep faith with him and helped get him back on his feet. Pooling whatever resources they had, they managed to raise $3,000 capital to start a new business. It was launched on 14 February 1876.

The business was registered as F. and. J. Heinz Company, the names being those of Henry's brother John and his cousin Frederick, both of whom had injected cash into the enterprise. Henry's name was not added because his bankruptcy legally prevented its inclusion. It would not in any case have served any useful purpose as it was too closely associated in the public's mind with failure.

Under the terms of the partnership agreement for the new company, Sallie would own half and the remaining half would be shared equally between John, Frederick and Henry's mother Anna. Although Henry was not officially part of the company, the family recognized it was his in all but name and were happy for him to be the driving force behind it.

With some eight acres of land still in the family's hands and with the additional forty-five acres that Frederick was able to rent, there was enough land for the cultivation of a substantial quantity of horseradish and cabbage. But Henry was careful not to make the mistake of growing his own cucumbers—the Woodstock experience was one he was determined never to repeat. He resolved only to buy them on the open market.

With little capital available, the embryonic business relied predominantly on its sales of horseradish to generate cash flow. And it was the Heinz women and children who provided the required labour to produce it, working long hours in the day and late into the night.

The factory regained

An opportunity to ease the pressure of work on the family presented itself quite unexpectedly when the owner of the factory in Pittsburgh, from which Henry had been evicted, heard of the company's rebirth. He immediately offered the factory for hire once more. With this at his disposal Henry could take on workers and would be able to speed up production. He could also extend his product range to include pickles, sauerkraut and vinegar. But there was a serious obstacle: he couldn't afford the rent. It was no doubt a rare moment of delight and relief in a year of intense struggle when the owner told him he could have the factory rent-free in the short term.

There was, however, another major obstacle: there was not enough money to pay the workers their full wages. However, Henry was able to persuade them to accept half-pay for a short period and to regard the other half as a loan with which he would buy essential equipment. He promised to reimburse the shortfall at a time agreeable to them.

The strain of rebuilding

He spared no energy in trying to rebuild the company. He had his finger on the pulse of every aspect of its operations, from cultivation and production to sales and accountancy. He regularly worked sixteen hours a day to keep on top of things and he had the added inconvenience of having to walk long distances because he couldn't afford a horse. Despite everything he did, his efforts to find customers often met without success and it was an obvious source of discouragement. Looking back years later he wrote: 'The physical and mental strain was enough to kill more than one man.'

Tomato ketchup launched

But he persevered and even began to think of ways of extending his product range. This was necessary if the company was to grow. A significant step forward was the introduction of tomato ketchup in the summer of 1876.

Making tomato ketchup was a task that women in the household disliked as intensely as grating horseradish. It was monotonous, repetitive work involving peeling, cutting, and removing seeds. Henry immediately saw the sales potential in removing this toil by producing the ketchup himself. He astutely advertised his new product as 'Blessed relief for Mother and all the women in the household'.

As with everything he produced, quality was his primary concern. He knew that any garden produce was only as good as the seed from which it was grown. He therefore took great pains to study seeds and ensure that only the best were sown. It was his declared aim to 'protect the customer by owning the product all the way from the soil to the table'. As no other commercial food processors were taking this trouble, the quality of his tomatoes was unrivalled. It was the foundation upon which the phenomenal success of Heinz Tomato Ketchup and Heinz Cream of Tomato Soup were built. Today the Heinz company processes over two million tons of tomatoes every year, more than any other company in the world.

Change of fortune

Henry's perseverance and relentless hours of toil paid off. By June 1877 the company's capital value had risen dramatically and by the end of the year profits had exceeded expectations. In addition to quality, a key element in the reversal of the company's fortunes was the immense respect he received for honouring his debts. Ever mindful of his 'Moral Obligations', he had begun to pay back everything he owed. Ironically, many of the customers who had deserted him in his hour of need were now themselves in financial difficulties because of the economic climate. They could not afford to pay him, yet to their amazement Henry graciously extended credit or, in some cases, even gave them items free of charge.

Henry's generosity of spirit was particularly evident in his attitude to former enemies. One of those, Joseph Wolfert, came to apologize for the way in which he had behaved towards him. Henry wrote in his diary that Wolfert 'was ashamed to come in'. However, on receiving a warm welcome at the door, Henry recalled, 'He was very much pleased and apologized for having persecuted me and slandered me. . . . I told him I forgive him for all, that these trials have done me good. We shook hands and I told him to call soon and bring his wife along.'

A wagon-builder who had made life as difficult as he could for Henry during his black period was another who hit on hard times himself. Things were so bad he had to sell his furniture to raise money. When Henry learned of this he promptly bought the furniture and arranged to have it delivered to the man's home as a gift. The two met shortly after on the street and when the wagon-builder saw Henry he went up to him, shook his hand and said: 'The man whom I treated as an enemy has proved to be my friend and saved me in my trouble.'

Henry's sense of honour in repaying his debts and his willingness to forgive made a deep impression on those who had shown little pity when he most needed their support. As a result he won many new friends and established a loyal customer base.

Establishing the brand

With a natural flair for marketing Henry found effective ways of establishing the Heinz brand in consumers' minds. In 1877 he introduced the keystone trademark. It was an astute choice because it immediately linked the company with the State of Pennsylvania of which the keystone is the emblem. It was also a powerful symbol because a keystone is the central wedge at the top of an arch holding all the other stones together. By association the Heinz name suggested strength and reliability.

Customers were already aware of Heinz products because of their reputation for quality but Henry realized he could reinforce the brand in the public's mind even further by enhancing the appearance of his products on the shelves of grocery stores. He familiarized himself with glass-making processes in order to produce bottles and jars that were uniquely shaped and visually appealing and he made them even more eye-catching by attaching colourful labels to them printed on high-quality paper. It was a very effective form of advertising. They immediately stood out from those of competitors who attached little importance to presentation. Furthermore, his salesmen were instructed to replace dirty labels on shelves with new ones, thus ensuring the brightness and attractiveness of Heinz bottles and jars. It was a policy that helped establish the Heinz brand as the market leader.

Embracing new technology

Another significant step in the company's growth was the adoption of new technology. In 1876 Henry and Sallie visited the Centennial International Exhibition in Philadelphia. It was the first official world's fair in the United States and was held in Philadelphia to mark the centenary of the signing of the Declaration of Independence in that city. The fair showcased the latest technological developments and two exhibits in particular caught Henry's eye: an automatic tin-canning machine and a pickle-sorting machine. They were just what he needed.

Cans were much more cost effective than glass or crocks as containers because they could not easily be broken. The visit to the fair prompted Henry to acquire a canning machine and by March 1877 one was in operation in his factory. Initially it turned out 55 cans an hour but within three years it had been adapted to increase the quantity to 120 an hour.

The pickle-sorter he bought was also a valuable addition. It was quite rudimentary at first but after some modification at the factory it could sort cucumbers by size into five different categories according to the type of container in which they were to be packaged. The advantage of this was that uniformity of size made the product much easier for grocers to sell.

Church and home life

Around this time Henry and Sallie joined Grace Methodist Church in Sharpsburg, a daughter church of the one they attended in Fifth Avenue in Pittsburgh. Sallie became active in charity activities at Grace Church, particularly in hospitals and in work with children, while Henry was committed to Sunday school teaching and temperance work.

The Temperance Movement—the fight against drink and the misery it caused—was very close to Henry's heart. He had seen the devastating effect of alcoholism on his brother Peter, who often ended up in prison because of it. Henry did everything he could to help Peter, giving him employment and taking him to temperance meetings. He always stood by him, despite the fact that he was an acute embarrassment to the family. It is hardly surprising, then, that Henry refused to sell any of his products to saloons and other places where alcohol was available. If he found any Heinz products on sale in such places, he promptly removed them.

As the company began to stabilize, Henry's personal life entered a more settled phase. His son Howard was born in August 1877 and entries in his diary during this period show an increasing interest in simple pleasures such as the company of his family, a picnic, a visit to the opera and church activities.

A month after Howard's birth the family moved from Sharpsburg to Pittsburgh so that Henry could be near to the factory to oversee operations. However, about eighteen months later they returned to Sharpsburg because Sallie had found the polluted Pittsburgh air intolerable and was concerned for her health.

Time out in Europe

By 1879 Henry had repaid his debts and restored the business to solvency. His diary entries for that year show a buoyancy and confidence that were to prove fully justified. Only a year later the company recorded its biggest-ever profits. Two years after that he could afford to buy the factory site.

In 1886, with the company now on a secure financial footing, Henry felt he could take a three-month break in Europe with Sallie, his four children, his sister Mary and his sister-in-law Lizzie Praeger. The main purpose was to visit relatives in Germany and with this in view he had already started German lessons the previous year. Although his parents were German, it was not the language he was brought up in because they felt they should speak the language of their new country at home.

In addition to visiting relatives, Henry also looked upon the European trip as a golden opportunity to establish new business links. He accordingly took a Gladstone bag of samples with him and five packing cases of Heinz products. He also went armed with a notebook to record any observations or ideas that might prove useful for his business. The party of eight sailed from New York in May for the eight-day Atlantic crossing to Liverpool.

After spending three days in Liverpool, they set off for London. On the way they stopped in Bedford, the birthplace of John Bunyan, author of *The Pilgrim's Progress*. Henry loved Bunyan's allegory of the Christian's journey through life and wrote that the book 'wielded an influence for good in the world that has never waned'.

The London experience

Henry and his party arrived in London late on Saturday, 12 June 1886 and stayed for two weeks. They visited many of the popular tourist sights including Buckingham Palace, the Houses of Parliament, the National Gallery and the British Museum, but Henry ensured that there was also a spiritual dimension to the trip. Their first day in London was a Sunday and he therefore wrote in his diary: 'This being Sunday, not forgetting our churchgoing habit, we all drove to the City Road Chapel, the most historic Methodist Church in the world. It was erected by John Wesley in 1778.'

Henry was a great admirer of John Wesley, the founder of Methodism, and Wesley's City Road Chapel is still recognized today as 'the Mother Church of World Methodism'. After the service he paid his respects at Wesley's grave behind the chapel and took a small pebble from nearby to take home as a token of affection. He and his party then crossed the road to the Bunhill Fields burial ground to visit the graves of Susanna Wesley (John's mother), John Bunyan, Isaac Watts, the renowned hymn-writer, and Daniel Defoe, author of *Robinson Crusoe*.

As a dedicated Sunday school teacher Henry was keen to compare the way in which lessons were taught in England with the way they were taught back home. He therefore paid a visit in the afternoon to a Methodist Sunday school in order to study the teaching methods and to make relevant notes.

One of the most memorable experiences of his life was the service he attended that evening at the Metropolitan Tabernacle, the biggest Baptist chapel in the country. It wasn't the size of the building that impressed him—it could hold six thousand people—but the inspirational sermon by Dr Charles Haddon Spurgeon, the chapel's minister and one of the most famous personalities of his day. During his lifetime Spurgeon preached to some ten million people and became renowned as 'the Prince of Preachers'. Wherever he preached, huge crowds flocked to listen. His powerful sermons are still read and appreciated today.

When the service was over, Henry was introduced to Spurgeon and was deeply impressed by him: 'He is the humblest, simplest, great preacher I ever met. A child can approach him.'

Of course, no tour of London was complete without a visit to Westminster Abbey, where England's kings and queens are crowned, and during his stay Henry attended a service there, too. Inside he took the opportunity to copy into his notebook the inscription on the memorial to John Wesley and his brother Charles, the great Christian hymn-writer.

Fortnum and Mason: first business link in Europe

Friday, 18 June 1886 proved to be an historic date in the Heinz company's history. That day Henry did the unthinkable: without an appointment or letter of introduction he made a direct sales pitch to Fortnum and Mason, the most prestigious supplier of quality food in England. This famous store, established in 1707, was frequented by the rich and famous and on its front at 181 Piccadilly were proudly displayed in gold letters the words 'Purveyor to the Queen'. This was the highest accolade any business in England could receive.

Disregarding the expected behaviour of salesmen, Henry ignored the service entrance and strode confidently through the main door sporting his finest clothes and a top hat. He looked every inch the refined gentleman. In his hand he held his Gladstone bag containing 'Seven varieties of our finest and newest goods', including horseradish and tomato ketchup. He asked to see the Head of Grocery Purchasing.

Such was Henry's distinguished appearance and presence that the Head of Grocery Purchasing was fully prepared to hear what he had to say. With very little difficulty Henry was able to persuade him to sample the products. The buyer was clearly impressed by them. To Henry's surprise and immense delight he said quite calmly: 'I think, Mr Heinz, we will take the lot.' It was the Heinz company's first breakthrough into a foreign market and from this small beginning the idea of 'The World our Field' took root. The company went on to operate with phenomenal success in international markets, enabling Henry to declare at a later date: 'Mountains and oceans do not furnish any impassable barrier to the extension of trade.'

Henry's two weeks in London were so enjoyable and made such a great impression on him that he returned there year after year.

To Germany

London was followed by a five-day visit to Paris and then it was on to Germany, his parents' country of origin. Henry was obviously keen to meet his relatives but that wasn't his only reason for visiting that country. His thirteen-year-old son Clarence was suffering from asthma and Henry had little faith in American doctors to cure him. He had decided, therefore, that the trip to Germany should include visits to doctors in Heidelberg for Clarence's benefit. He was also concerned that Sallie should have treatment for her rheumatism and he arranged for her to visit the renowned Bavarian spa town of Bad Kissingen.

Chapter 5

Henry travelled extensively in Germany. He had an insatiable thirst for knowledge and took detailed notes on many aspects of German life, including farming methods, road-building and the educational system. As a devout Christian he never failed to attend church on Sundays and he made notes comparing the different forms of service. A particular highlight was his visit to the church in Wittenberg where Martin Luther had started the Protestant Reformation in 1517.

He was also keen to deepen his understanding of German business practice, visiting a range of factories to study manufacturing methods and training programmes. His visit to the country's biggest chocolate manufacturers, the Stollwerck Brothers in Cologne, was particularly satisfying. It resulted in an agreement with the company to distribute Heinz products in Germany.

The way the Stollwerck company treated its six hundred employees made a deep impression on Henry. They were provided with exceptional facilities and services to make their working conditions as pleasant as possible. Although he was already treating his own employees well, Henry now felt he should do much more for them and he took home ideas that he would later implement in developing the harmonious worker relations for which the Heinz company would become famous.

Henry concluded his visit to Germany with a few days in Kallstadt, Bavaria, where his father was born. The visit to the family homestead was a happy one. He recorded in his diary: 'Seventy-four years ago Father was born in this . . . large, commodious home built in the 14th century. . . . I rested well in the old home. . . . Arose joyfully, calling to memory many incidents connected with the family. As near as we could count, we find a total of over 100 relatives in Kallstadt.' Henry was delighted to establish contact with so many relatives and often returned to the area to visit them.

The vacation in Europe had been immensely rewarding but it had a tragic ending. On arrival in New York Henry was met with the sad news that his twenty-five-year-old brother Jacob was ill in Philadelphia with typhoid fever. He immediately brought Jacob home but he died within a week. More sadness followed. Just a few months later his thirty-one-year-old sister Margaret also died.

H. J. Heinz Company launched

Despite the pain of his bereavements, Henry continued to work tirelessly to develop his business. Under his dynamic leadership it continued to grow and prosper although he often drove himself to the point of exhaustion in taking it forward.

But this could not be said of his brother John, whose lack of effort became an increasing source of frustration to Henry, prompting him to write: 'The more I take on, the more John slackens up.' John's shortcomings were also recognized by other members of the family and he was finally given two options: either run a branch of the company on his own or sell his one-sixth share and walk away. He chose to sell. On John's departure the other partners unanimously elected Henry president and on 1 November 1888 the name of the business was changed to H. J. Heinz Company. This was now legally possible because the restriction on the use of his name due to his earlier bankruptcy had expired.

Although the business was flourishing, Henry knew he needed to increase production if it was to develop further. To achieve this, he had to build a new factory close to accessible rail links. He found a site by the Allegheny River in Allegheny City, about half a mile from Pittsburgh's business quarter. His plan was to build a complex of some seventeen buildings that not only incorporated state-of-the-art machinery and fittings but were also visually attractive. The exteriors would be in the Romanesque architectural style and many of the interiors would contain stained-glass windows, marble walls and red mahogany woodwork. For ease of cleaning and to ensure the buildings always looked presentable, brick faces would be glazed and floors would be laid of hard varnished maple.

Henry wasted no time in getting the project up and running. By August 1889 the first of the buildings had been completed. He personally supervised construction, ensuring that only the finest-quality bricks, wood and tiles were used. At times he even helped the bricklayers with their work, passing bricks up to them when needed.

Of course, Henry's vision for a grand factory complex was extremely costly. One building was complete but sixteen more were planned. How, then, did he find the necessary financial means to carry the project to completion? It was because of his incredible flair for publicity that he managed to boost sales and win an ever-growing army of customers. He seemed to know instinctively how to capture the public's imagination with unusual, sometimes even dramatic, forms of advertising. The following examples give an insight into the originality of his thinking.

The 'pickle pin'

The first was an ingenious solution to an irksome problem at the World's Columbian Exposition in Chicago in 1893, the world's fair which celebrated the 400th anniversary of Christopher Columbus's arrival in the New World. The Heinz company had been allocated space for a display of its products on the second floor of one of the two hundred exhibition buildings. But the exhibition site covered some 600 acres (2.4 km²) and involved a considerable amount of walking. With countless attractions to choose from, it was quickly apparent that visitors easily missed the Heinz company's display.

Furthermore, it was a deterrent to have to ascend forty-four stairs to reach it. Henry was understandably frustrated at the low footfall on his floor but how could he increase it when there were countless more easily accessible ground-floor attractions in other buildings?

He hit on a revolutionary idea. He enlisted the services of local boys to drop thousands of small white cards throughout the site. On them was printed an invitation to receive a free souvenir on presentation of the card at the Heinz exhibition. Intrigued, thousands made their way there, wondering what they would be given. Very quickly the building was in danger of collapse. Police had to regulate the crowds while the supports of the second floor were strengthened to accommodate the weight of the army of visitors. And what was the free gift they received? A rubber pickled gherkin, about 1¼ inches long, displaying the name HEINZ. It could be attached to clothing as a lapel pin or brooch or attached to a watch chain as an ornament.

The 'pickle pin', as it was called, captured everyone's imagination and about a million were given away. Such was the impact of this novel gift that exhibitors on the ground floor, whose displays were ignored in the rush to get upstairs, sued Henry for unfair competition. However, the exhibitors on the second floor who had benefited from the high volume of traffic that boosted their visitor numbers, threw a dinner in his honour and presented him with an inscribed silver cup.

Henry saw the 'pickle pin' as a significant marketing device and as a result formulated the principle: 'Let the public assist you in advertising your products and promoting your name.' The idea was so revolutionary that years later, Arthur Baum, editor of the renowned Indianapolis journal *Saturday Evening Post*, called the pin 'one of the most famous give-aways in merchandising history'. Henry's ground-breaking marketing concept has been adopted ever since as normal business practice.

The '57 Varieties' slogan

Three years later, in 1896, Henry had another inspired idea—one with which his name has become synonymous. He was travelling on the overhead railway in New York when he noticed an advertisement in the carriage for '21 Styles' of shoe. It struck him that he, too, had a variety of products so why not state the number in his advertising? But what was that number? He explains how he arrived at it:

> Counting up how many we had, I counted well beyond 57, but '57' kept coming back into my mind. 'Seven, seven'—there are so many illustrations of the psychological influence of that figure . . . that '58 Varieties' or '59 Varieties' did not appeal at all to me as being equally strong. I got off the train immediately, went down to the lithographer's where I designed a street-car card and had it distributed throughout the United States. I myself did not realize how highly successful a slogan it was going to be.

Henry's account contradicts the widely held belief that he chose 5 because it was his lucky number and 7 because it was Sallie's. Interestingly, in 1930 the company produced the *Heinz Book of Salads* listing what it considered to be the definitive 57 products.

Henry was so convinced of the marketing power of the '57 Varieties' slogan that within a week he had placed advertisements with the image of a green pickle accompanied by those words in newspapers and on hoardings.

However, he was not satisfied to use only familiar vehicles of advertising such as newspapers and hoardings to make his slogan known; he wanted much more eye-catching ways to make it unforgettable. With a flair for the dramatic, he had the huge white concrete number 57 carved into hillsides in some of the USA's most prominent locations, such as San Francisco Bay. He also rented fields next to railway lines in order to erect large concrete

57s or to hang huge tomatoes displaying this number. Additionally, he had some four hundred Heinz-owned freight wagons painted bright yellow with the name Heinz and the number 57 prominently displayed on each side in giant green characters.

His bold ideas worked. Today '57 Varieties' is synonymous with the name Heinz. In fact, it has been so successful that the expression '57 Varieties' has even passed into popular usage to suggest anything that consists of many varied parts.

The Heinz Pier, Atlantic City

Another of Henry's imaginative marketing ideas was the purchase in 1898 of the Atlantic City iron pier on the USA's East Coast. Atlantic City was an immensely popular holiday hot-spot with visitors from across the USA and Henry saw its pier, which extended some nine hundred feet into the sea, as an ideal vehicle for promoting his brand.

He bought the pier and had it fully remodelled. At each side of the entrance, which was in the form of a huge Roman triumphal arch, he placed a giant replica pickled gherkin. At the opposite end of the pier he erected a glass pavilion mounted with a seventy-foot electric sign beaming out the words 'Heinz 57 Varieties'. It earned the pier the nickname 'the Crystal Palace by the Sea'. The pavilion showcased thousands of bottles and cans of Heinz products and visitors were invited to sample anything they liked without obligation to buy. They were also offered a free pickle pin and free Heinz postcards to send to family and friends.

The pier fully justified Henry's expenditure. After just one year, the company's sales increased by 30 per cent. By 1944, when unfortunately it was destroyed by a hurricane, the pier had attracted a remarkable total of some fifty million visitors.

A happy workforce

Henry's advertising flair was undoubtedly a key factor in the phenomenal growth of his company and of his increasing personal fortune. By 1896 he was a millionaire. By 1898 all seventeen buildings of his factory complex were complete. It was the largest factory of its kind in the world.

But Henry never forget the company's humble beginnings. In 1904 he moved his house in Sharpsburg where the business had started in 1869 to a specially chosen site within the new factory complex. It was towed on an enormous barge some five miles down the Allegheny River. It served as the company's museum there until 1953 when it was presented to Greenfield Village, a 200-acre (0.8 km²) open-air museum in the Detroit suburb of Dearborn. It was one of nearly a hundred historical buildings of great significance in American history that were moved there from their original locations. The Heinz house displays exhibits highlighting the company's innovative business practices and marketing techniques.

As well as never forgetting the company's humble origins, Henry was ever mindful of his responsibility for the well-being of his workforce. Inspired and challenged by the care he had seen for the workers at the Stollwerck factory in Cologne, he did everything he could to ensure the best possible working conditions for his own employees. He provided them with rest and recreation rooms, dining facilities, locker rooms, dressing rooms, reading rooms, libraries and a five-storey building for recreational purposes with a hall large enough to seat up to 1,500 people. The hall was used for dancing, musical and dramatic performances, films and lectures. Employees could further enjoy lunchtime concerts and daily park rides in a horse and carriage.

Additional facilities provided for them were a swimming pool, a gymnasium, roof gardens and a hospital. Henry attached great importance to health and he made available free of charge the services of a doctor and nurse for general health problems not connected to the workplace. In addition, he provided a dentist and introduced free life insurance. Heinz employees were also given generous time to recharge their batteries. Unlike workers in a number of other factories who worked seven days a week, Heinz employees were not required to work Saturday afternoons or Sundays.

Despite his genuine care and concern for his employees, Henry was not a soft touch. He was a disciplinarian who expected wholehearted commitment and high moral standards from his workers. He would not tolerate drinking or swearing and he would instantly sack any male employee who made inappropriate remarks to a female worker.

But even in cases of dismissal, he showed he had a heart. On one occasion, when an employee was found to be the worse for wear for drink, he was given a warning that a second offence would result in dismissal. The man re-offended and Henry immediately instructed that he should be sacked.

When he was informed that the offender was penniless and his wife and child were in hospital, it made no difference. The dismissal was to stand. But Henry quickly added: 'That's business. The other matter is charity. Draw the necessary money and look after the wife and child.'

At the Paris Exposition in 1900 and the St Louis World's Fair in 1904 Henry was awarded gold medals for the quality of his care for his workforce. Significantly, there was never a strike at his works during his lifetime.

But it wasn't just his workforce that Henry cared for. He also had great compassion for the poor and homeless and did what he could to help them. One of his diary entries is significant: 'We fed 43 tramps and beggars during the month of January. . . . The majority we sat to the kitchen table and gave them coffee and warm victuals as it was very cold. We gave some of them work so as to earn money for their lodging.'

Priorities

By 1900, H. J. Heinz had become the biggest food processor in the world and by 1910 was the USA's largest international company. Already a millionaire in 1896, Henry was a multi-millionaire in 1910. But his business success was never at the expense of his priorities as a Christian. He was always conscious of his accountability to God for the use he made of the gifts he had been given. Regarding his use of time he stated in a public address: 'We are responsible to the Maker and Giver of time as to how we use it.' And with regard to money, he urged: 'Make all you can honestly; give all you can wisely.'

He followed his own precepts. He expended huge amounts of time and vast amounts of money in the promotion of Sunday schools, believing passionately that 'the Sunday school is the world's greatest living force for character building and good citizenship'. He readily acknowledged his own debt to it: 'In my own life the Sunday school has been an influence and an inspiration second only to that of a consecrated mother.'

International Sunday school leader

When Sallie died from double pneumonia in 1894 aged only fifty-one, Henry was devastated. He threw himself into his work but it was his faith and increasing involvement in Sunday school organizations that carried him through and helped him to emerge from his grief. A year after Sallie's death he became a director of the Pennsylvania State Sabbath School Association, eventually being elected President. In 1902 he became a member of the Executive Committee of the International Sunday School Association and two years later of the Executive Committee of the World's Sunday School Association. He was appointed its chairman in 1913. He served the Sunday school movement for a total of sixty-four years right up until his death.

In 1913 he organized a five-month tour to the Far East visiting more than seventy cities to introduce Sunday schools to China, Japan and Korea. He personally paid for all the Bibles that were to be distributed and he paid most of the costs of the travelling party of thirty.

The first country on their itinerary was Japan where they spent a month. Although Christianity was the faith of only sixty thousand of Japan's population of fifty-two million, Henry's reputation as a world-renowned manufacturer opened many doors. The party visited several major cities where they were warmly received by mayors and other dignitaries. They were even guests of the Prime Minister at a specially arranged evening dinner.

Japan proved to the most receptive of the countries they visited. Remarkably, by the time of Henry's death six years later in 1919, there were some two hundred thousand Japanese Sunday school members.

Death and legacy

At the age of seventy-four, after a life of devoted Christian service and of spectacular business achievements, Henry died at his home in Pittsburgh on 14 May 1919. As with Sallie, double pneumonia was the cause of his death. His funeral took place at East Liberty Presbyterian Church, Pittsburgh, where he had worshipped after moving into the area in later life. There is a stained-glass window in the church as a memorial to him. After the service he was laid to rest in the family mausoleum in Homewood Cemetery. Poignantly, a representative of Japan's two hundred thousand Sunday school members made the long journey to Pittsburgh to lay a wreath at his tomb.

At the time of his death his company was one of the foremost in the world and it has continued to grow ever since. When Henry coined the '57 Varieties' slogan in 1896, he could never have dreamt that the number of Heinz products today would be not far short of six thousand. Sales are phenomenal. One and a half million cans of Heinz Baked Beans are consumed daily in the UK while across the world 650 million bottles of Heinz Tomato Ketchup are sold annually. Global yearly sales of single-serve ketchup packets amount to a staggering eleven billion. In business terms alone, Henry has left a considerable legacy.

Yet remarkably, in view of his phenomenal business success, Henry was not seen primarily as a businessman by his contemporaries. In the obituaries that appeared in the press following his death, he was defined first and foremost as a 'churchman'. His quality of character and the countless hours and huge sums of money he had devoted to church and Sunday school work throughout his working life had clearly made a much deeper impression. But it is often in very simple ways that we learn most about a person. The heartfelt words of one of Henry's own workers are as richly informative in their sincerity and brevity as many an obituary: 'I have lost the best friend I ever had.'

It is evident that Henry's faith as a Christian was the defining characteristic of his life. In the opening of his will he ensured it was also unmistakable at his death:

> I desire to set forth at the very beginning of this Will, as the most important item in it, a confession of my faith in Jesus Christ as my saviour. I also desire to bear witness to the fact that throughout my life, in which there were the usual joys and sorrows, I have been wonderfully sustained by my faith in God through Jesus Christ.

He bequeathed generous amounts to hospitals and social service organizations but not surprisingly his largest bequests were to Sunday school associations. He also left $100,000 (about $1½ million today) to endow a Chair of Sunday School Education at the University of Pittsburgh.

Throughout his life Henry's Christian faith and his business practice were inseparable. One was an expression of the other. Perhaps, then, there is no better way to finish than how we started—with the words of E. D. McCafferty who knew him so well:

> One often hears it said that a business man, at least one who deals with other than small affairs, cannot be a Christian. It is affirmed that there is an irreconcilable incompatibility between the principles of business and the teachings of Christ. The life of such a man as Mr. Heinz is an answer to that theory. He made a success of his business; he made a success of

his Christian living. There was no lack of harmony between them. His Christian life was a help in his business. His business enabled him to make his Christian life effective in ways of practical service to others.

JAMES KRAFT, cheese pioneer

The name Kraft instantly brings to mind the word 'cheese', yet cheese was just the launchpad for one of the biggest food and beverage companies in the world today. The company has, in fact, marketed countless other products in more than 170 countries. Twelve of its brands alone have achieved annual sales of at least $1 billion worldwide, while total annual net revenues have reached $34 billion.

Yet James Kraft, the man who gave birth to this vast business empire, did not consider business to be his priority: 'I would rather be a layman in the North Shore Baptist Church than to head up the largest corporation in America. My first job is to serve Jesus.'

This is a side of Kraft that will come as a surprise to many but it is not the only thing about him that might be surprising: he was also an authority on American jade gemstones and an accomplished jewellery-maker. He was a man of many talents. His story is fascinating and inspiring.

Canadian upbringing

Although renowned as a successful American entrepreneur, James Lewis Kraft was, in fact, Canadian. He did not become a naturalized United States citizen until he was in his thirties. He was born on 11 December 1874 on a dairy farm about fourteen miles from Niagara Falls in the small community of Stevensville, now part of Fort Erie, Ontario. He was of German extraction, his surname originally being spelt Krafft until he decided to drop one of the 'f's later in life.

He was the second of eleven children, eight boys and three girls, born to George and Minerva Krafft. They were Mennonites, members of a religious group formed in German-speaking countries during the Protestant Reformation in the sixteenth century. Because of repeated persecution over the centuries, Mennonites were often forced to leave their homelands.

Chapter 6

Many emigrated to Pennsylvania, USA, where James's grandfather Francis Krafft lived before moving to Stevensville to start the dairy farm on which James grew up.

James attended school in Airline Street, Stevensville, but in out-of-school hours he helped on the farm. As the area has remained agricultural, the farm can still be seen close to the junction of Bowen Road and Winger Road. Among his numerous tasks he ploughed the fields with a hand-guided plough, which was such hard work that it gave him calluses. He also milked the cows and, significantly, he learned how cheese was made. This knowledge was to be crucial in launching him into a career in cheese production for which he would become world famous.

James's childhood was a happy one, despite money being tight. There was a close bond between all the members of this large family. His mother, he said, was 'much harassed' with so many children to look after but she always managed to keep the house neat and tidy. Although he described her as 'gentle' she would correct her children's bad behaviour by firmly tapping them on the head with the thimble she always wore on the stump of a finger she had lost in a farm accident.

'The kindly eye doctor'

James fondly recalled an event in his childhood that had a profound and lasting effect on him. Until he was fourteen, he suffered continually from blurred vision and excruciating headaches. He assumed this was normal and that he simply had to put up with it. He recalled: 'Near-sightedness was so acute and distressing that I assumed everyone suffered continuously from furious headaches, and that all the earth had the blurry image of a boat seen from under water.'

But this completely changed one day when he was tending to the horse and washing the buggy of a holiday-maker who spent each summer on the shore of nearby Lake Erie. The man happened to be an eye specialist and quickly noticed that James was struggling with his vision. He told him he needed to wear glasses and that he could buy a pair in Buffalo, the town just across the border in the USA. When James explained that his parents couldn't possibly afford them with so many mouths to feed, the kind-hearted specialist bought them for him: 'The kindly eye doctor gave me back the earth and all that was in it, completely in focus and beautiful beyond anything I could have dreamed. . . . The look of the hills, the road, the streams, even of the people . . . as they walked, took on definite lines instead of a blur.' James was overwhelmed by the specialist's generosity and never forgot it: 'I cannot think of another act of human kindness during my lifetime which can compare with his.'

Stranded in Chicago

Four years later, aged eighteen, he successfully applied for a position as an assistant in Ferguson's general store in nearby Fort Erie. He worked there ten years, gaining invaluable experience in the retail trade and making many useful contacts. In 1902 one of those contacts arranged for him to work in Buffalo in the offices of the Shefford Cheese Company. Although there were good rail and ferry connections between Fort Erie and Buffalo which were separated by the Niagara River, James decided to move into the American town to save time and travel costs. It was an important step on his career path.

He clearly made a very good impression at Shefford's because after only a few months he was sent to Chicago to run the company's office there. However, for reasons unknown, things didn't work out and he lost his job. At twenty-eight he found himself alone in Chicago with only $65 in his pocket. What could he possibly do stranded in that big city with very little money? But adversity is often the gateway to opportunity and the challenging situation in which he found himself served as the trigger that released his entrepreneurial instincts.

Opportunity in adversity

He had long been aware that Chicago grocers raced to the city's warehouse district at daybreak every day to be first in line to get the pick of the cheeses. The grocers knew that the later they arrived, the poorer the quality of the available remaining cheese would be, making resale very difficult. They found it frustrating and inconvenient to be involved in this early morning stampede to the market. James quickly realized that their frustration and irritation presented him with a golden opportunity to generate an income for himself. He could save them considerable time and money by buying wheels of cheese himself and delivering them directly to their stores.

Using the little cash he had, he rented a horse and buggy and each morning at the crack of dawn headed down to South Water Street to

Chicago's biggest cheese market. He knew exactly what to look for. From his experience of watching cheese made on the Stevensville farm, from selling it in Ferguson's store and from working for Shefford's, he could immediately distinguish between good and inferior-quality cheeses. He was also aware of the volatile nature of cheese and why it was so important to get the freshest. It was a highly perishable product and when it lost its freshness it would quickly start to melt. He simply had to be first at the market to get his deliveries to the stores before they opened. Any later and the cheese would have started to deteriorate.

It was an excellent business idea but he hadn't taken into account a very serious limitation. He was just a one-man operation and it wasn't physically possible to secure the custom of enough grocers quickly enough to get his name known and establish a reputation as a wholesaler. Inevitably this proved to be a mountain too hard to climb. His first year was a disaster and ended with a loss of $3,000, a substantial amount at the time.

A life-changing revelation

After one particularly bad day he sat down dejectedly by his buggy and his beloved horse Paddy. Like many animal-lovers who often talk to their pets, he turned to Paddy and told him how low in spirit he felt. In his outpouring of despair, he unexpectedly became aware of a deep inner voice. He felt it was telling him that in his struggle to create a successful business he had left God out of the equation. His relationship with God was wrong and needed to be put right. He recognized the truth of what he heard. Turning to Paddy, he said: 'Paddy, there is something wrong. We are not doing it right. I am afraid we have things turned around and our priorities are not where they ought to be. Maybe we ought to serve God and place Him first in our lives.'

The revelation had a life-changing effect on him. Professor Hiley Ward of Temple University, Philadelphia, to whom James told the story, later recorded: 'From that day Kraft dedicated his life fully to Christ and sought His guidance in all his endeavors.'

James's Christian faith gave him a new perspective, new priorities and renewed energy. The struggle to make ends meet didn't suddenly go away but after his spiritual awakening he approached it in a completely different spirit, confident that God would guide him in the path he should take.

Launch of J. L. Kraft & Bros. Company

In the course of the next six years James slowly but surely managed to establish a reputation for trustworthiness and reliability for his wholesale service which won him an ever-growing number of customers. By 1905 he had taken the bold step of selling the cheese he carefully selected at the market under his own brand name—Elkhorn Kraft Cheese. It was unusual at the time for manufacturers to risk attaching a brand name to their products because they feared it would acquire a negative association and cost them sales if quality fell below customers' expectations. James, however, was inspired by the example of Oscar Mayer, a Chicago businessman who sold meat under his own name with great success, and he was confident that he, too, could establish a brand that would become synonymous with quality.

And he was right. As his reputation for supplying quality cheese grew, his brand name earned respect and his business thrived. With the support of his brothers Charles, Frederick, John and Norman it had become strong enough by 1909 to be incorporated as J. L. Kraft & Bros. Company with James as president. 'What we say we do, we do do.' became the company's motto.

Marriage to Pauline Platt

The year 1909 was a landmark year for James for another reason. On 2 June he married Pauline Platt, a native of Catonsville, Baltimore, where she was born on 21 August 1886. Pauline was living in Chicago when James met her. Shortly after their wedding they joined the North Shore Baptist Church on Chicago's North Lakewood Avenue, with which they were to have a long and fulfilling association. Their marriage was also to be a long and happy one. Pauline, in fact, lived to the ripe old age of one hundred. They were to have one child, a daughter Edith.

The problems of waste and taste

After the company's incorporation it continued to go from strength to strength. This was, of course, largely due to its reputation for quality, trustworthiness and reliability, but effective advertising also played an important part in its growth. In 1911 the Kraft name began to appear on Chicago's overhead trains and on billboards around the city while circulars were regularly mailed to storekeepers. In 1912 an office in New York City was opened and two years later, in 1914, the company acquired a factory 130 miles east of Chicago in Stockton, Illinois, where it began the production of its own cheese. By the end of 1914 Kraft was selling thirty-one varieties of cheese across the United States.

For all the success James was enjoying, he was troubled like all cheese producers by two seemingly insoluble problems: waste and inconsistent taste. Waste occurred in two main ways. The first was at the point of sale. The most popular cheese at the time was Cheddar and it sat on store counters in the form of 60-pound wheels under a protective bell-shaped glass jar. Whenever a customer wanted to buy a portion, it was cut as a wedge from the wheel leaving exposed edges that quickly dried out. These edges were sliced off and thrown away before the next wedge was cut, an immensely frustrating situation for storekeepers because the discarded off-cuts reduced saleable quantities and potential profits.

Waste was an ongoing problem but it was even worse in the summer months. Most retailers had no means of refrigeration and refused to sell cheese between June and September when it quickly turned mouldy and developed a vile smell. Furthermore, lack of refrigeration meant it could only be transported over short distances. It just couldn't survive long journeys.

Another serious problem was variation in taste. Cheeses were mostly produced on individual farms and sold to wholesalers. It was highly improbable, therefore, that a Cheddar produced on one farm would taste exactly the same as a Cheddar produced on another. Even in factories there could be inconsistencies in taste from one day to the next. Sometimes the cheese might be too strong, other times not strong enough. And while in stores, the taste would gradually change in the course of its shelf life.

Frustrating research

James was determined to find a way of prolonging the shelf life of cheese. Ironically, should he be successful, he risked a possible reduction in sales. Quite simply, the longer the cheese lasted, the less often retailers would need to buy in new stock from him. Clearly this did not seem to be a consideration as he searched for a solution.

He made a little progress in overcoming the problem through the use of protective packaging. From 1914 he began selling portions of cheese in glass jars or tinfoil. This was not only much more convenient for storekeepers and their customers but also reduced the amount of wastage caused by dried-out wheel edges. But it was no more than a partial solution. Although useful for sales in small quantities, it was no answer to the problem of bulk sales. James could not let go the conviction that an answer was waiting to be found and he began experimenting in his apartment with a large copper pot.

He knew that bacteria were instrumental in the ripening process that turned milk into solid masses (curds), separating these from the liquid (whey). But he was equally aware that these same bacteria were also destructive. If they were not killed at the right time the cheese would continue to ripen and eventually rot. But how could he kill them before they destroyed the cheese?

He felt certain that the most effective way to stop deterioration was to fill the pot with Cheddar cheese, heat it to a certain temperature then stir the cheese until it was bacteria-free. Over several years he put this theory to the test, trying a range of temperature levels, stirring for varying lengths of time and stirring at different speeds. He also tried all these operations in varying combinations, but to no avail. The result was always the same: a foul-tasting gluey mass. In the face of so much frustration he must often have felt like giving up.

Breakthrough achieved

His dogged determination and perseverance were finally rewarded when he achieved the elusive breakthrough quite by chance one night in 1915. With the temperature of the pot set at 175°F, his mind began to wander with the monotony of stirring. After fifteen minutes he suddenly realized he had been stirring longer than intended, stopped, then examined the cheese. To his utter amazement it was perfect. Replication of the experiment using the same formula confirmed the result. He knew beyond any doubt that he had discovered the secret not only of preventing cheese from spoiling but also of achieving a consistent taste. It could even be shaped in various ways without detriment. This was the defining moment of his career.

The market leader

The revolutionary new process he had discovered led to his product becoming known as 'processed' cheese. It was launched in August 1915 under his brand name Elkhorn Kraft Cheese and sold in 3½ and 7¾ ounce tin cans. They flew off the shelves in the USA and, with transportation over long distances now possible, found a ready market in India and Asia. Within a year export sales had risen from $5,000 to $150,000. By the end of 1915 J. L. Kraft & Bros. was the largest dairy company in the USA. Wary of imitators, James applied for a patent to protect his invention. It was awarded on 6 June 1916.

In 1917 the USA entered the First World War and by the time of the Armistice in November 1918 some two million American troops were stationed in France. These troops had to be fed and it was essential to find food products that could be transported in huge quantities over long distances without spoiling. Processed cheese was ideal for this purpose. By the end of the war the US government had purchased some six million pounds in weight of Kraft cheese. The revenue from these war-time sales accelerated the company's already meteoric growth.

Hostility and opposition

However, despite its enthusiastic reception and runaway success, processed cheese did not meet with universal acclaim. It was condemned, not surprisingly, by rival cheese-producing companies. They dismissed it in numerous press articles as being an inferior product, claiming it was not real cheese at all. Kraft had altered the very nature of cheese itself, they argued, and in consequence his product should correctly be renamed 'embalmed' cheese.

The objectors partially won their argument. The issue was addressed by federal authorities who ordered that cheese modified in this or any other way must be designated 'processed cheese'. But unhappily for Kraft's opponents, this seeming victory proved to be hollow when researchers at the University of Wisconsin found that two-thirds of the people in their investigation much preferred the taste of processed cheese to that of natural cheese.

Expansion

No amount of hostility or opposition could slow down the company's growth. Factories were opened in twenty-three states and Edam, Gouda and blue cheese were added to Cheddar in the product line. In 1919 a specialist advertising department was established, with James taking a leading role. That year Kraft became the first cheese company to launch a national advertising campaign, targeting national women's magazines. They initially advertised in black and white, with the first Kraft colour advertisement making its appearance in a national publication within two years.

In 1920 a major investment was made with the purchase of the A. F. MacLaren Imperial Cheese Company of Toronto. It was a strategic acquisition, giving access not only to the Canadian market but also to MacLaren's operations in Europe and beyond.

This was a dynamic period and by 1923 sales had reached $22 million, making Kraft the biggest cheese company in the world. A year later it opened its first international office in London and was listed on the Chicago Stock Exchange under its new name The Kraft Cheese Company.

Giving God his due

James did not take the astronomical growth of his company for granted. He attributed it to God's guidance in answer to prayer at each important new step he took. He only proceeded on any course of action when he was sure he was on the path to which God had directed him. As he explained: 'When I have a problem, I pray about it, and what comes to mind and stays there I assume to be my answer. And this has been right so often that I know it is God's answer.'

In gratitude to God for the guidance and blessings he received he donated a large percentage of his personal profits to Christian organizations. It gave him great joy to know that his monetary gifts were a significant help in the development and growth of the Christian causes he supported. He commented: 'The only investment I ever made which has paid consistently increasing dividends is the money I have given to the Lord.'

One of the beneficiaries of his generous giving was Chicago's Northern Baptist Theological Seminary which prepared students for Christian ministry. This institution was particularly close to his heart. He was a trustee and provided many scholarships for its students.

He also gave generously of his time and money to the North Shore Baptist Church in Chicago. He helped with administration and served as a deacon. He was regularly at the church door to warmly welcome visitors to the Sunday morning services. He taught in the Sunday school for over forty years and in time became superintendent. Pauline, too, served as a Sunday school teacher.

'The touch of Christmas life'

James firmly believed that the expression of God's love in a Christian should not be limited to specific acts of generosity or to a particular time of year. In a letter he wrote just before Christmas 1924 to Deacon Harley Ward of Chicago he explained that the spirit of goodwill characteristic of the Christmas season should be perfectly normal for a Christian at all times:

> In my work and in the business of life, I mean to try not to be unfair or injure any man. . . . Without pretense, and in plain words, good-will is what I mean, in the spirit of Christmas. . . . There are a great many people in the world . . . to whom . . . we cannot very well send a Christmas gift. But there is hardly one, in all the circles of our acquaintance, with whom we may not exchange the touch of Christmas life.

The principle of goodwill and 'the touch of Christmas life' were evident in the treatment of his workforce. He had great respect and affection for his employees and over the years got to know literally thousands of them by name. During the Second World War he personally wrote to each one who served in the armed forces. His employees, in turn, loved him, always referring to him affectionately as 'Mr J. L.'

'Kraft's was a great place to work,' was the comment of many of its employees over the years. 'It was like a big family,' said one former employee. 'He gave a lot of meaning to people's lives because of the way in which the company was run,' said another.

'My first job is to serve Jesus'

James's amazing success as a businessman was not achieved without obvious passion for his work and without a huge commitment in terms of time and energy to developing his company. But his business life never consumed him or deflected him from his priorities. At the opening of this story we quoted his frank and direct statement exemplifying this: 'I would rather be a layman in the North Shore Baptist Church than to head up the largest corporation in America. My first job is to serve Jesus.'

There were no doubt times when his commitment to his church was challenged by his business pressures but he never wavered in his foremost loyalty. This was particularly evident in 1927 when the Kraft company, already the market leader in the USA, was involved in intensive negotiations to expand its international activities by establishing market footholds in Europe. James played a leading part in these negotiations and could take satisfaction from a successful outcome: a sales office was opened in Hamburg and the Kraft Cheese Company was established in London.

In the midst of these pressures he was invited to take on the position of Chairman of the Board of Deacons at his church, knowing full well that the role would make great demands on his time and energy. He would be required to chair regular meetings of the deacons, assist with pastoral ministry and help with the running of the church. He willingly accepted these responsibilities as a long-term commitment, serving wholeheartedly and faithfully in this role until his death twenty-six years later.

It was through prayerful consideration of his priorities and careful management of his time that James managed to combine his business commitments and church responsibilities without detriment to either.

Philadelphia Cream Cheese

By 1928 his company was employing ten thousand people and selling a million pounds of cheese in weight daily. Kraft's market strength increased even further after its acquisition of the Phenix (not Phoenix) Cheese Corporation that year. This corporation was renowned for its Philadelphia Cream Cheese, a product that had been created in 1872 by William Lawrence, a dairyman from New York State.

Like many other dairymen, Lawrence had been making his own version of Neufchâtel, a popular French cheese, but he came up with a completely original formula when he added cream to the recipe. The result was a delicious mild-tasting soft cheese that he initially simply called 'cream cheese', but in 1880, purely as a marketing device, he gave it the name Philadelphia Brand Cream Cheese. Lawrence had no connection with that city but it enjoyed an excellent reputation for fine-quality food. He felt it would enhance the appeal of his own cheese if it were associated in the public mind with a name synonymous with food quality.

In 1903, the Phenix Cheese Company of Cooperstown, New York State, bought Lawrence's business and the rights to the Philadelphia trademark.

Phenix, in turn, was acquired by Kraft in 1928 and the expanded company began trading under the name of the Kraft–Phenix Cheese Corporation.

As a Phenix-owned product, Philadelphia Cream Cheese had quickly suffered spoilage but now, with Kraft's expertise and experience on hand, it was modified and its shelf life extended. This considerably increased the product's market appeal and, in turn, the company's annual sales figures. In 1930 they exceeded $86 million. Forty per cent of the cheese consumed in the United States was now produced by Kraft–Phenix.

Merger with National Dairy

The thriving Kraft organization caught the eye of Thomas McInnerney, a Chicago pharmacist and founder of the Delaware-based National Dairy Products Corporation. McInnerney had built up National Dairy through the steady acquisition of strategically placed businesses across the country. In one year alone in the 1920s he acquired eighteen companies. His policy was to inject investment capital into the companies he bought but allow them to function autonomously under their own names and with their own personnel. In 1930 National Dairy employed some thirty-five thousand people and had sales of $374.6 million. It was by far the largest food products company in the USA.

When James was approached by McInnerney with a proposal for a merger, he responded positively. He already had it in mind to extend the Kraft product line and with investment from National Dairy this would be possible. It was a mutually beneficial arrangement enabling Kraft–Phenix to expand and National Dairy to take a substantial share of the profits. On 12 May 1930, the merger went ahead.

Creation of 'Miracle Whip'

Ever forward-looking, James had begun in the 1920s to explore opportunities for diversification and during that period he bought five mayonnaise-producing companies. With new capital available after the merger with National Dairy he decided to launch three new products— Kraft Mayonnaise, Kraft Thousand Island Dressing and Kraft French Dressing.

But it was the wrong time. The country was in the grip of the Great Depression and mayonnaise and other salad dressings were a luxury that few could afford. Furthermore, the production of mayonnaise was a hit-

and-miss affair—its taste and consistency could not be guaranteed. The sales department were adamant there was no future in this direction and made their feelings perfectly clear to James, but he refused to be dissuaded. He firmly believed there was a potentially huge market for mayonnaise if the problems of production could be overcome. He had been down this route before with cheese; he was prepared to go down it again with mayonnaise.

The only possible solution to the problems of taste and consistency, he was told, was the invention of a machine capable of measuring the ingredients to a high degree of accuracy, blending them into a fine mixture and maintaining the same quality of output each production run. James wondered how he could come by such a machine. It was a seemingly impossible challenge to create one. The answer arrived quite unexpectedly at the North Shore Baptist Church.

In conversation with one of the members of his Bible class, Charles Chapman, James learned that Chapman had invented a most unusual dual-purpose machine. It served as a tea trolley but could also wash dishes. James was impressed by Chapman's imagination and inventive ability and commissioned him to design the mayonnaise-making machine he needed.

Chapman rose to the challenge. Although it wasn't easy and took a lot of time he eventually managed to create a machine that produced not only the right-quality mayonnaise but additionally a salad dressing far superior in quality to any other that existed. Chapman's achievement was remarkable but the best was still to come. He discovered that by whipping the mayonnaise and the salad dressing together an amazing new product with a distinctive delicious taste was created.

James was absolutely delighted by the discovery. He was convinced this new product was a market-winner, not just because of its wonderful taste but also because it was cheaper than mayonnaise. At a time when household budgets were very stretched it was a significant selling point. But what should it be called to intrigue customers and make it sound appealing? By virtue of the fact that Chapman's machine had been described as 'miraculous', the new product was given the name 'Miracle Whip'.

Confident that Miracle Whip was something very special, James excitedly announced at the company's January 1933 sales conference that it would generate record sales figures, but his bold claim was unceremoniously dismissed with boos of disapproval. What was the sense of trying to sell yet more mayonnaise in the present climate, he was asked, when existing stocks could not be shifted? But he stood his ground. He declared not only that production would go ahead but that a million dollars would be invested to advertise it. It was a very brave decision in the face of such strong opposition.

Launch at the Chicago World's Fair

James wasted no time. Production started immediately and after two weeks of successful market trials, Miracle Whip was launched in May 1933 at the World's Fair in Chicago known as 'A Century of Progress International Exposition'. Located on a three-and-a-half mile site along the shore of Lake Michigan, it was organized to celebrate the city's centenary and to showcase major international developments in technology. It was the biggest architectural project in the United States during the Great Depression featuring, among many other attractions, magnificent displays in huge exhibition halls constructed in daring new styles. The fair received massive coverage in national newspapers, magazines and newsreels. What better place to unveil Miracle Whip, James felt, than at a venue constantly in the whirl of publicity and visited by millions?

The fair was initially scheduled to run from May to November but proved so popular that President Franklin D. Roosevelt persuaded the organizers to reopen it the following year. Over the two years that it ran, it attracted almost fifty million visitors. Dramatic events such as the arrival on 26 October 1933 of the Graf Zeppelin, the 776-foot hydrogen-filled German airship famous for providing the world's first commercial transatlantic air passenger service, attracted further huge media interest. Even a United States postage stamp was created to commemorate its appearance at the fair.

In the context of all this buzz and excitement James realized it was essential that the Kraft exhibition in the Foods and Agriculture Building should be a match for the attractions visitors could marvel at elsewhere on the site. He did not fall short. The centrepiece of the Kraft display was a giant non-stop Miracle Whip-making machine housed in a glass-enclosed air-conditioned room. Visitors watched in amazement. Word about the incredible new product the machine produced spread like wildfire and stores were quickly overwhelmed with the demand for it. Miracle Whip just flew off the shelves. James must have been delighted that his judgement had proved correct—by the end of 1933 Miracle Whip had become the top-selling salad dressing in the United States.

Innovative radio advertising

The impact of Miracle Whip was so remarkable that to maintain the sales momentum it was decided to offer a 'double-your-money-back' guarantee to any dissatisfied customer. To promote this offer the company decided to use radio as a vehicle for publicity, a major step forward from its print advertisements and in-store displays. James approached the leading advertising agency in the country, the J. Walter Thompson Company, to explore the best possible approach. The result was the creation of a musical variety programme, the Kraft Musical Revue, hosted by Paul Whiteman, leader of one of the most popular dance bands in the United States during the 1920s and 1930s and renowned as 'the King of Jazz'. Kraft commercials would be scheduled to appear during the show.

This two-hour weekly programme was first broadcast on 26 June 1933 in the New York metropolitan area and in New England. It was a huge success and within just two months of its launch was ranked by the Association of National Advertisers as one of the four most popular programmes on radio. It was soon airing on fifty-three major radio stations each week.

James had given much thought to the timing and presentation of the commercials. He was concerned that they might be swallowed up within the programme and overlooked. To prevent this, he had to ensure they had a distinct identity and appeared in a format that would make them stand out. To maximize their impact he decided to feature a single product instead of a variety. The commercials would appear at a point where there was a natural break in the programme and would be presented by an announcer not connected with the entertainment. It was a simple but effective formula. The commercials helped fix Kraft products firmly in the public mind and had a positive effect on sales.

The following year, 1934, the programme changed its name three times, eventually becoming Kraft Music Hall. By now the Kraft name had huge pulling power and during the sixteen years that the show ran it was hosted by some of the biggest names in show business. These included Bing Crosby, whose recording of 'White Christmas' is the best-selling single of all time, and Al Jolson, the highest-paid and most famous entertainer in the USA in the 1930s. Jolson is best remembered today as the star of the first feature-length talking movie, *The Jazz Singer*.

Not only were the show's hosts household names but so, too, were some of the guests it attracted over the years. Among them were top international recording artists such as Nat King Cole and Peggy Lee.

The dinner winner

James was always open to new ideas and when his St Louis sales manager showed him a packet of macaroni attached with elastic bands to a packet of Kraft Grated American Cheese on sale there, he was intrigued. It was the idea of a macaroni salesman who was promoting these two products as an ideal combination for a convenience meal. James was impressed. He realized at once what the enterprising salesman was doing: he was using cheese to help sell macaroni. James quickly saw that this could also work in reverse: that macaroni could help sell cheese.

He spoke to his brother Norman about the idea but Norman dismissed it as a gimmick. Undeterred, James then consulted Marye Dahnke, director of the Home Economics Department. Marye's response was wholly positive and she shared James's enthusiasm. She felt she could create a recipe using macaroni and cheese as the key ingredients and set to work on it. The successful outcome was a tasty product named Kraft Macaroni and Cheese Dinner that could be packaged in a single cardboard box. It made its market appearance in 1937 and, not surprisingly, it was the recently recruited St Louis macaroni salesman who spearheaded the launch. It was marketed as a 'A meal for 4 in 9 minutes' and was an instant success. Within just twelve months one million boxes had been sold. James's entrepreneurial instincts had once again proved themselves to be reliable.

Like Unto

However much business matters occupied him, James's Christian faith was always in the forefront of his mind. To him, life could not be packaged in distinct segments, faith being one of them. He saw the whole of life as a spiritual journey and everyday occurrences as reminders of deeper realities. A series of events on a boat cruise with Pauline and Edith in Florida in 1939 inspired him to write a book to make this point. It was written as a Christmas gift for his friends and not sold commercially.

His experiences on the cruise were richly instructive and he was grateful that 'many new lessons were learned, and many old lessons were learned anew'. These lessons were presented in the form of twenty-two parables illustrating Christian principles. The book's title, *Like Unto*, is a phrase James borrowed from the translation of the Bible into English authorized by King James I of England in 1611 (the King James Bible). This version is still much loved and widely used today, even though some of its vocabulary and expressions are no longer in regular usage. 'Like unto' was the translation of words used by Jesus when he spoke in parables to make analogies between daily life and the kingdom of heaven. One example is Matthew 13:45–46: 'the kingdom of heaven is like unto a merchant man, seeking goodly pearls: who, when he had found one pearl of great price, went and sold all that he had, and bought it' (KJV).

For many years James, Pauline and Edith had wanted to cruise on the quiet rivers and inland lakes of Florida. Their dream was finally realized in 1939 when a friend offered James the loan of his boat. The 48-foot-long vessel, *Gypsy*, was ideal for the purpose with a draught shallow enough to navigate the low waters of the region. It was also large and comfortable enough for a long 1,500-mile journey.

With Captain Green at the helm and accompanied by their cook, Frank, the Krafts started their voyage at the port of Jacksonville in north-west Florida. Shortly after setting out on the three-hundred-mile stretch down the east Florida coast, things started to go wrong. First there was a delay when a broken clutch had to be repaired. Next, a buoy used by sailors as a navigation mark was ripped from its anchor chain by a violent storm and drifted some distance away from its proper position. James takes up the story: 'the pilot, having no knowledge that the buoy had drifted, steered by its false position and thus the *Gypsy* ran aground. There she remained fast until high tide permitted her to float free and proceed.'

This incident gave him the cue for a spiritual parallel:

> The anchorless buoy is like unto many a false signpost along the straight and narrow channel leading to success. A young man embarking on a career fixes his ambition upon a distant goal, his path extending along the straight line of honesty, truth and Christian principles. But as he proceeds, the way seems far, and certain men persuade him that the anchorless buoys which they themselves pursue lead straighter to his

goal. And if the young man should deviate from his course, should fail to follow the hard and fast rules of navigation by instruments which he knows to be sound, he will find to his despair that he has been deceived and led to his destruction.

After leaving the coast and proceeding along the St Lucie River, they sailed into Lake Okeechobee, where they were once again hit by a violent storm. The ship was tossed to and fro while the passengers inside were thrown around mercilessly. James was deeply impressed by the calm way Edith reacted to the terrifying situation. She fully recognized the danger they were in but refused to panic, taking heart from a break in the ugly black sky where the sun was shining through. She knew this meant the storm would soon pass. Inspired by his daughter's calmness, James wrote: 'She was like unto the Christian man or woman who, living in this stormy world filled with black wars and rumours of war, with strife and clouds of doubt descending all about, still looks upon the light from heaven, calm in the faith that light will disperse the darkness.'

On another occasion they dropped anchor at Matecumbe Key, an island just off Florida's south coast, to look for fresh water but found none. Fortunately there was a spring on nearby Englishman Island, so called because it was owned by a Londoner. This kind-hearted Englishman had made his spring freely available to anyone who needed water and *Gypsy* was able to stock up. James saw a parallel in the Bible (Acts 17:16–31), prompting him to write:

> It is like unto the story of the Apostle Paul who, when he journeyed to the city of Athens, found the Athenians worshipping many gods. Whereupon he stood on the top of Mars Hill and declared to the great concourse of people, in substance, as follows: I perceive you are very religious and worship many gods, yea, even an unknown god, but I am come to declare unto you the only true God in all the universe who is able to give unto you the sustaining water of life which is free for the taking.

These are just a few of the incidents recorded in the book that opened James's eyes to things he had not previously noticed or had simply taken for granted. He regarded both the cruise and the lessons he learned as gifts from God.

The move to television

James's open-mindedness and readiness to embrace new ideas were qualities he showed right into his seventies. His age did not stop him running his business with the same inventiveness and mental agility that were characteristic of his earlier years.

In 1945, now seventy, he changed the name of the business to Kraft Foods Company to reflect its ever-expanding product line. Two years later he moved into an entirely new field of advertising: television. Although the sale of food products to the armed forces during the Second World War had made the company's already very strong financial position even stronger, James was convinced that television would help Kraft Foods achieve still further growth.

Inspired by the success of the company's radio programme, Kraft Music Hall, James was convinced that a similar format would work for TV. He proposed an hour-long live series that would feature comedies, dramas and adaptations of classics such as *Alice in Wonderland* and *A Christmas Carol*. As with the radio programmes, he planned that commercials for Kraft products should appear at strategic points in the TV shows.

The Kraft Television Theatre, the first commercial programme on network TV, was duly launched on Wednesday, 7 May 1947 and transmitted on an experimental basis in the New York metropolitan area. To gauge the impact of the medium as an advertising vehicle, one of Kraft's barely known products, MacLaren's Cheese, featured in the commercial breaks in the earliest shows. It had received hardly any publicity prior to its TV appearances. Would these make a difference? They did. The cheese was an instant success and as a result further Kraft commercials were shown to great effect on the company's TV shows.

The programme went from strength to strength. From its launch in 1947 until the final episode in 1958 nearly seven hundred shows were produced, running continuously without a summer break. It launched the careers of many actors, directors and playwrights. One example is Hope Lange whose appearances on Kraft Television attracted the attention of a Hollywood producer who signed her to appear alongside Marilyn Monroe in the film *Bus Stop*. Lange was later nominated for an Oscar. Not only did the programme discover new talent, it also attracted world-famous names such as James Dean, Grace Kelly and Paul Newman. Not surprisingly, therefore, it set new audience viewing records.

The commercials shown during the programme were in the form of live cooking demonstrations. As it was assumed that the mother of the family was the cook in the household the demonstrations featured female hands. These became known as 'The Kraft Hands' and the advertising slots as 'The hands commercials'. To ensure that the viewer was not distracted by looking at anything other than the hands the demonstrator was not seen and a male voice explained what the hands were doing. The voice was that of Ed Herlihy, a well-known radio announcer in the USA from the 1930s to the 1950s. He served as 'The voice of Kraft' for more than forty years.

The 'hands' formula proved to be extremely effective. In one instance, when the demonstration of a clam dip made with Philadelphia Cream Cheese was shown, grocery stores ran out of stock of canned clams within just two days. And the take-up for a recipe booklet featured in the same show was 500 per cent higher than expected.

Much of the credit for this success goes to Marye Dahnke, the director of the Home Economics Department. Marye, it will be remembered, had created the recipe for Kraft Macaroni and Cheese Dinner. She served the company for almost forty years, establishing a reputation for hosting 'cheese talks' across the country to promote Kraft cheese. She was also the author of the popular *Cheese Cookbook* published during the Second World War. Marye was just the person with the right expertise to provide 'The Kraft Hands' with delicious recipes to prepare on screen. In the eleven and a half years of the Kraft Television Theatre's existence, she created enough recipes to cover the near seven hundred programmes. There is little doubt that her inventiveness contributed significantly in establishing new Kraft products as household names.

Adventure in Jade

Remarkably, in the midst of his hectic business activities and important church responsibilities, James managed to find time for a hobby: collecting jade gemstones and making jewellery from them. In fact, he even achieved a national reputation for his knowledge and expertise in this field and published a book on the subject in 1947 called *Adventure in Jade*. All royalties from the book were given to charity.

Knowing that many people would be surprised that a successful businessman could find time for a hobby, he wrote: 'I learned long ago that a man cannot do his best work in any sort of commerce unless he is able, at any moment, to turn his mind away from his business and its problems completely.'

In his book James traces his passion for jade and jewellery-making directly to the man he described as 'the kindly eye doctor' who bought him a pair of glasses when he was fourteen and enabled him for the first time to appreciate 'the wonder of the world in focus'. Until that time he could barely distinguish objects he unearthed when ploughing, but with glasses a whole new magical world opened up to him: 'ploughing the east pasture with my new eyes wide open, I began the treasure hunt that has led me to a lifetime of adventure, an eternity of pleasure, an occupation of hand and heart and spirit that has never left me for a moment'.

For the first time he was able to identify and appreciate 'the early chips of agate and quartz, the Indian arrowheads and other treasures of unspeakable worth which I uncovered'. He actually considered his short-sightedness a blessing in disguise because, unlike those blessed with good eyesight, he did not take the beauties of the natural world for granted: 'I perhaps had something of an advantage over many boys and girls,' he said. He felt he had received the gift of 'wonder'.

The Indian arrowheads James uncovered awoke in him a fascination for ancient American history and he began to collect primitive axes, tools and stone bowls. This, in turn, prompted him to collect pieces from ancient China crafted from jade.

Jade lacked the great commercial value of its more illustrious peers diamond, ruby, sapphire and emerald but to James it was 'the most various and beautiful of all the stones on earth' and he loved searching for it in its natural environment. But it was not an undertaking for the faint-hearted. It was usually found in inaccessible, often dangerous places. In specifying the qualities needed of someone prepared to venture into 'high, cold, hazardous, lonely spots', James unwittingly described aspects of his character that were also evident in his business career: 'rugged, enduring, adventurous, pioneering, incurably curious, tireless'.

His search for jade stones was mostly concentrated in America although he did on occasions travel as far afield as China. While searching in

Wyoming he discovered one of the largest pieces of jade rock in existence. It weighed 2,495 pounds and was later exhibited in the Chicago Museum.

He enjoyed the company of like-minded jade enthusiasts and wrote: 'Through the years, pursuing my hobby wherever it led me, I have always tried to meet friends along the road, to seek out men with similar interests, to write to them, to know them, and to travel along the way with them.'

The jewellery-maker

As well as the excitement of searching for jade, James also loved fashioning it into jewellery. It was a task, he said, that needed 'patience, resourcefulness, imagination', again qualities characteristic of him as a businessman. He never felt that the hours he spent in his workshop were wasted, even when his finished pieces were sometimes faulty: 'Anything you learn about the nature of stones as you work with them—and about yourself as a workman during the process—is knowledge gained and adventure sustained.'

James's hobby was never a mere self-indulgent pleasure and he freely gave pieces he had crafted to others: 'My jade had to be shared—and I wanted to share it as far and wide as I could.' He made a jade pin for each member of the choir of his church and he loved to reward excellence in his company by presenting outstanding employees with beautiful polished jade stones that he had personally cut and set into rings.

To receive one of these rings from the much-loved and highly respected Mr J. L. meant something. They are still treasured today as family heirlooms by the children and grandchildren of their recipients. Even fifty years after James's death when a *Chicago Tribune* columnist, John Kass, published an article dismissing his hobby as eccentric, former employees rose to his defence. Kass, instead of being offended, was greatly impressed and wrote: 'Kraft people from across the country pestered me with angry emails. They referred to him as Mr J. L. They revered him. That bond, that sense of responsibility between employee and boss, has been lost in modern American business.' This wholly unexpected response from former Kraft employees made such an impression on Kass that he was moved 'to find out more about this interesting man'. Clearly, good people's lives can still speak volumes after their deaths.

Another beneficiary of James's skill was the North Shore Baptist Church. He had funded the building of a new chapel within the church and he personally adorned it with a magnificent east-facing window 6½ feet high and 3½ feet wide which he crafted from 446 pieces of different coloured American jade. Its centrepiece is a large cross made of the rarest white jade. This beautiful window is a wonderful sight as it catches and reflects the sunlight.

James took great pleasure in creating jewellery with a personal touch but it gave him particular joy to design special pieces for Pauline as an expression of his love for her. Fittingly, then, *Adventure in Jade* is dedicated to her: 'This book is for PAULINE KRAFT whose patience with her husband's time-consuming hobby is enduring; whose forbearance is surely beyond that of all other women; and whose jewel box contains, if not the richest gems in the kingdom, certainly those wrought with the greatest affection.'

Kraft Cheese Slices

James lived long enough to preside over one more major development in the company's history. It was the appearance of cheese slices on the market in 1951.

It had long been obvious that customers found it difficult to cut cheese into slices of a constant size and thickness. The result was not only irregular shapes but also broken pieces and curled ends. Obviously pre-cut slices would prevent these problems but at the current stage of technological development this could not be done. Cheese could only be cut when cold but in the manufacturing process it was packaged in its hot, liquid state. Some way had to be found of cooling it ready for slicing.

It was James's brother Norman, now head of Research & Development, who achieved the breakthrough. He developed a machine in which hot, liquid cheese was channelled through a giant rolling pin. This 'chill roll' as it was called cooled the cheese and transformed it into a long ribbon ready for slicing into three-inch squares. These, in turn, were assembled into packets of eight ready for sale. Initial market testing proved positive and so, in 1951, Kraft De Luxe Process Slices were launched nationally and given maximum exposure in Kraft Television Theatre commercials. The public loved the new slices and grocers were soon reporting increases in cheese sales by as much as 150 per cent. Within a year they had become the most successful product the company had launched to date, breaking all its previous sales records.

Chapter 6

This latest surge in the company's exponential growth must have given James great pleasure and satisfaction. He must no doubt often have looked back to those early days when he was struggling to make a living with a horse and buggy and marvelled at how far he had come. And he would have acknowledged with humility and deep gratitude God's clear guidance at every stage of his business career that enabled him to achieve so much.

Death and legacy

James lived another two years after the successful launch of the cheese slices but on 16 February 1953 he suffered a heart attack and died. He was laid to rest in the Memorial Park Cemetery in the north Chicago suburb of Skokie not far from where he and Pauline lived.

He had lived a richly varied and deeply fulfilling life. His marriage of more than forty years to Pauline had been a very happy one, his business had enjoyed success beyond his wildest dreams and he had established a national reputation as an authority on jade. But never far from his mind was the guiding principle of his life: 'My first job is to serve Jesus.' He would have been delighted, therefore, that on a commemorative plaque unveiled in Fort Erie in 2003 to honour his achievements, his Christian faith was also highlighted.

His memory lives on, not only in the marvellous products he created but also in his outstanding example as a man of the highest calibre. He was a brilliant businessman, a caring employer and a loving husband and father. He enriched the lives of thousands in his time and his story can still inspire us today.

ANTHONY ROSSI,
Tropicana juice giant

Wen twenty-one-year-old Anthony Rossi arrived in the USA from his native Sicily, he had virtually nothing but he eventually founded a company that was to become the leading fruit juice producer in the world. An exceptional businessman and a brilliant inventor, his success was spectacular but it is only part of his story. As the inscription on an American university building so succinctly puts it: 'Anthony Rossi lived to honor God.'

Birth in Sicily

Anthony Talamo-Rossi was born on 13 September 1900 in Messina, Sicily, the fourth of seven boys in a family of nine children. Their parents, Adolfo and Rosaria Talamo-Rossi, were owners of a successful department store in Messina.

The family lived in considerable affluence but it did not last. The store closed in 1905 after the inept handling of its finances by Adolfo's father-in-law and as a result the family lost their home. But three years later, in 1908, a much greater disaster struck the family. A horrific event occurred that devastated eight-year-old Anthony and set him on a spiritual journey that defined the rest of his life.

The Messina earthquake

On Monday, 28 December at 5 a.m. the Rossis, now living on the third floor of a modest apartment block, were suddenly awakened by a loud rumbling sound. A dreadful earthquake was about to hit the city. As the building began to shake the family raced downstairs to the protection of the sturdy stone arch over the main entrance. They made it just in time. The building collapsed all around them but the arch remained intact. Terrified, they huddled under the arch waiting for the earthquake to pass.

After twenty minutes the tremors stopped and the Rossis anxiously looked for a way out of the shattered city. All around them were scenes of utter destruction. Gaping holes and crevasses in the streets, as well as mountains of rubble, made movement almost impossible. Darkness, rain and outbreaks of fire caused by broken gas pipes added to the chaos.

More was to come. The earthquake's epicentre was in the Strait of Messina which separated Messina from the Italian mainland. Some ten minutes after the tremors had subsided a forty-foot-high tsunami swept across the harbour towards the city, flattening any buildings still standing. Two further tsunamis followed, both higher than the first. The nightmare seemed to be never-ending.

The disaster made headlines across the world. It was the most powerful earthquake ever to strike Europe, reaching 7.1 on the Richter Scale. Its effect could be felt almost two hundred miles away. More than 90 per cent of Messina's buildings were destroyed including almost everything in the historic centre.

Tragically, even worse than the loss of its buildings, Messina lost almost half its population that morning. Among the 75,000 dead was Anthony's much-loved twelve-year-old brother Riccardo who had been staying with relatives. Anthony was devastated. He could not come to terms with the loss of his brother. This traumatic experience triggered an agonizing search for answers to questions about life and death and heaven and hell, questions that troubled him for years.

Evacuation

The situation in Messina was desperate. The Italian army and navy raced to the scene to search for survivors and treat the injured, bringing with them essential provisions and medical supplies. As all railway lines in the area had been destroyed and roads were impassable, evacuation by sea from the earthquake zone was the only option.

Three days after their home had been flattened—and having had nothing to eat during that time—the Rossis were among five hundred refugees picked up by a Russian ship and taken eighty miles down the coast to Syracuse. For the next eighteen months they would be housed in makeshift barracks.

After the earthquake, the population of Messina dropped from 150,000 to 19,000, these being the survivors who chose to live among the ruins.

Evacuated families gradually began to return, among them the Rossis in 1910. Once again they were housed in makeshift barracks.

A troubled mind

Despite having fun with new-found friends in the barracks community, Anthony's mind was deeply troubled. He desperately wanted to know how he could be certain of going to heaven where he believed Riccardo to be. Growing up in a strong Catholic household he attended Mass regularly, served as an altar boy and recited the prayers of the rosary with his grandmother, but all these efforts failed to ease his anxiety.

When an adult acquaintance convinced him he would go to heaven if he recited a set number of prescribed prayers each morning and evening for seven years, Anthony eagerly seized on the advice. He followed this path diligently day after day, not just for seven years but for seven more. It didn't help. He still felt lost.

The businessman is born

Anthony's spiritual search in those early years was accompanied by the first signs of a talent for business. In 1911 his father was working as the manager of the city hospital and the family had moved into accommodation within the hospital grounds. Next to their house was an acre of land still buried under debris from the earthquake. But Anthony could see beyond the rubble—he firmly believed this site could become a market garden.

With the encouragement and help of the hospital's eighty-year-old gardener, Santo Bombaci, he began clearing the site. It was a formidable task for an eleven-year-old and an octogenarian but after months of back-breaking work, the first vegetable seeds were planted. Anthony also grew many rows of onions. He knew he could sell them but he was also aware that his father would never let him. He therefore asked a friend to take bunches to the market and offered him a percentage of any sales he made.

The onions sold well. Although Adolfo never discovered what his son was doing, he unwittingly brought the enterprise to an end. When hospital visitors gasped at the abundance of onions in the garden Adolfo invited them to take as many as they wanted as the family couldn't possibly eat so many themselves.

Chapter 7

The lure of America

In 1915 tragedy struck the family once again. After a year-long fight against cancer, Anthony's mother died at the age of only thirty-nine. It was a terrible loss for the fifteen-year-old boy. She left another gaping hole in his life to add to that already left by Riccardo.

Soon after Rosaria's death, the family received a visit from a relative living in the USA. He had come to Sicily hoping that the warm climate would help him to recover from a stroke. Anthony asked him question after question about America and his imagination was fired by what he was told. It planted a seed in his mind that would later bear great fruit. He resolved to go there one day.

Military service

That dream was a long way off and in the meantime Anthony had to earn some money. His first job was as a trolley bus conductor but in 1917, aged seventeen, it finished when he was conscripted to the infantry in the Italian army. This was during the First World War but fortunately Anthony did not see front-line action as he was assigned to guard duties at the government palace in Rome.

Although hostilities ceased with the armistice of 11 November 1918, Anthony's military service continued for another three years. During the whole of this period his dream of going to America grew in intensity and when he left the army in 1921 his mind was made up. He would start a new life in the USA.

Arrival in New York City

Twenty-one-year-old Anthony said his farewells to his family and headed for Naples to board a ship for New York City. He had nothing more than two suitcases and $30. Unable to speak English and with no qualifications he could justifiably have felt worried but the opposite was the case. In later years he vividly recalled: 'It was exciting, exciting.'

Although he knew no one in New York City he had been given the name of a contact living in Thompson Street in a friendly Italian neighbourhood in Manhattan. This would be his temporary base. He was warmly welcomed there but soon afterwards a job in a machine shop and a room with an Italian family on West Broadway were arranged for him.

Taxi driver and chauffeur

Anthony enjoyed his job in the machine shop and worked overtime to increase his weekly income. After just six months he had saved enough to buy a second-hand Buick. He loved driving around in it and became so familiar with the streets that he decided to start a business as a taxi driver. He exchanged his Buick for a Renault and did so well that he was able to send money home to Messina to help support the family.

Aged twenty-two, he now started to think of bigger things. Taxi-driving was enjoyable but he knew he could make better money as a private chauffeur. From his savings he paid $250 for a second-hand Cabriolet and although it did not look too impressive in its present state he managed to considerably improve its appearance.

He found employment as chauffeur to the chairman of the Hudson & Manhattan Railway Company on a salary of $450 a month. It was a challenging job. Mr Root was cold, aloof and highly eccentric. He avoided any kind of conversation with Anthony, communicating instructions via a series of signals with a bell. He would ring once to start or stop, twice to turn right and three times to turn left. His strange behaviour extended to wearing white gloves when reading a newspaper to keep his hands free from print.

Anthony's duties consisted of taking the chairman to his office at 1.15 p.m. and back home from his office at 4 p.m. five days a week. At weekends he drove him around Central Park or down Riverside Drive to enjoy views of the Hudson River. On Friday evenings in the autumn and winter he would take him to collect a lady friend he wanted to escort to the opera.

The mornings, as well as the hours between taking his employer to work and bringing him home, were Anthony's own. He filled them by doing more taxi-driving to boost his income. In addition to the Cabriolet for his chauffeur duties, he had acquired two further cars to develop his taxi business.

The grocery business

Somehow he found time for another sideline. With the help of his elder brother Joe who had joined him in New York he collected fresh eggs from the nearby countryside and sold them door to door in the big city. They proved such a hit that local grocery stores began to place orders with him.

This encouraging contact with grocers stimulated Anthony's fertile entrepreneurial mind and in 1927 he decided to open a store of his own. He found an ideal corner site in Jackson Heights on Long Island, sold his chauffeur and taxi businesses and opened the Aurora Farms grocery.

He took great pride in the appearance of his store, the range and quality of his goods, his fair prices and the quality of his service. The store proved very popular and his business thrived. Only two years after it had opened the Wall Street Crash of 1929 plunged the country into the deepest recession it had ever known but even during this troubled period Anthony's business prospered. He continued with it well into the 1930s but then felt ready for another challenge. He sold the store for $30,000 and bought a restaurant.

His new enterprise started promisingly but it saddened him that only a year after he had left the grocery it stood empty. The owner had failed miserably. Overcome with nostalgia, Anthony handed the restaurant business over to Joe and promptly bought the store back.

Marriage to Florence Stark

It was an excellent decision. Not only did he restore its fortunes but he met his future wife there. He was immediately smitten by Florence Stark when she first came into the store. Born in 1892, she was the daughter of a Methodist minister and worked locally as the secretary of a respected inventor. The ever-imaginative Anthony found a novel way to get to know her. When she left her box of groceries with him while she shopped in another store, he craftily made it heavier by hiding jars of jelly among the items she had bought. When she couldn't lift the box, he offered to deliver it to her home. The plan worked and it was the start of a courtship that led to their wedding.

The grocery business flourished and Anthony moved into larger premises further down the road where he opened a self-service supermarket, only the second in New York City.

Spiritual hunger

Although he had found a loving wife and developed a thriving business in New York, two things unsettled him. First, as a Sicilian accustomed to the warm Mediterranean climate, he found the New York winters unbearably cold. He yearned for the warmth and sunshine in which he had grown up. Secondly, deep spiritual questions triggered by Riccardo's death still gnawed away at him. He did not have peace of mind.

There was an easy solution to the first problem. He asked Florence how she would feel about moving south to the warm, sunny climate of Florida. She liked the idea and they decided to leave. Of course, Anthony needed to find work there and he began to explore the possibility of farming.

The obvious place to find information was the magnificent New York Public Library at the junction of 5th Avenue and 42nd Street. It had one of the finest collections in the world. He was about to start reading a book on tomato-growing when he noticed another book on the table—*The Life of Christ*. The title drew him like a magnet. He opened it and started reading. Once he had started, he couldn't put it down. The effect on him was so profound that he decided to forget books about farming and read the Bible instead.

His spiritual hunger was insatiable. Day after day he returned to the library working through the Bible from beginning to end. He was enthralled by what he read and became certain of one thing: there was real hope for him. Having lived in terror at the prospect of judgement and hell, the words of John 3:16 stopped him in his tracks: 'For God so loved the world that He gave His only begotten Son, that whoever believes in Him should not perish but have everlasting life.'

He now began to think of God in a more personal way even though he did not yet have the inner peace he craved.

Tomato farmer in Florida

Anthony had taken a positive step forward on his spiritual journey but he also had to give careful thought to the next step in his career. The pull of farming had become irresistible and in 1940 he and Florence spent a year growing and selling tomatoes in Cape Charles, Virginia, before moving to Bradenton on Florida's west coast. There they acquired a rented fifty-acre farm to start a tomato business.

Anthony hired a team of men to work with him but was soon criticized by other employers for the high wages he paid. This put them under pressure to do likewise. He refused to back down and rode their hostility.

When the crop was ready for harvesting, he realized he had left it too late to hire enough pickers. His lack of experience was costly. Competition for pickers was fierce and most had been snapped up by other farmers long in advance. As a result, much of Anthony's crop was left in the ground and went to waste. Despite this setback he still managed to finish his first year with a profit of $5,000, and, learning from his mistake, went on to make much greater profits in subsequent years.

The Floridian Cafeteria

Having established a successful tomato business, Anthony's sense of adventure once again prompted him to look for another challenge. This time, however, he asked God for guidance. Determined to grow spiritually, he had joined the First Methodist Church with Florence in Bradenton on their arrival in 1941. Although his understanding of the Bible was still very basic, he knew enough to believe that God would direct his path if asked.

He felt God's guidance could not have been clearer. One day, out of the blue, a friend came over to him in town and pointed to a self-service restaurant—The Floridian Cafeteria—on the corner of 6th Avenue and 12th Street. He told Anthony it had just come on the market. Anthony took one look at it and instinctively felt it was for him. He bought it for $8,000. He invited Joe, currently working as head chef at a major Chicago hotel, to take charge of the cooking side. Refurbishment of the cafeteria started at once. The new look and the fine food began to attract an ever-growing number of regular customers, not just from Bradenton but also from Sarasota thirteen miles away. In fact, The Floridian became so popular that diners had to wait patiently in a long queue for Sunday lunch.

This wasn't the only noticeable characteristic of Sundays at The Floridian. In a most unusual departure for a cafeteria, Anthony arranged a regular devotional time in the morning with the services of a pastor. And, as another expression of his growing Christian faith, he refused to serve alcoholic beverages. This had no ill effect on the business, however. At the end of the first year it had made a net profit of $35,000.

The Terrace Restaurant, Miami

The Floridian flourished and Anthony began to forge ambitious plans for expansion. With the start of a chain in mind, he bought The Terrace

Restaurant in Miami in July 1944. Situated in a popular tourist location on Miami Beach, it seemed the ideal place for him to start his chain. With a seating capacity of five hundred and a thriving coffee house, it was the biggest restaurant south of Washington DC. He and Florence promptly moved to Miami to run the new enterprise.

As with The Floridian, refurbishment was the first step. The interior was substantially improved and a dance floor was built. It was an exciting moment when the doors first opened. But in his enthusiasm Anthony had failed to consider one crucial factor: the USA was at war. Petrol rationing was in full force and had a crippling effect on the tourist industry in Florida. Visitor numbers plummeted and restaurants were seldom full. The Terrace began losing $1,000 a day. In a desperate attempt to reverse his losses, Anthony abandoned one of his principles—never to serve alcoholic beverages. He tried to ease his conscience by only allowing them at the table. He would not provide a bar. In his heart of hearts he knew it was a feeble compromise and it made him feel uncomfortable.

It didn't work. In fact, things went from bad to worse. Very soon all his savings disappeared and in a last-ditch effort to save the restaurant he sold The Floridian in Bradenton for $35,000. This, too, had no effect. A month later that money had gone. Only five months after buying The Terrace, he was faced with total ruin. Just $3,000 was left in the bank and there was no way he could meet bills for $18,000 due in the next few days.

Anthony took a good look at himself. He knew he had betrayed his conscience when he allowed alcohol to be served at the table. How could he possibly expect God's blessing on his business when he had abandoned one of his moral principles? He deeply regretted what he had done and vowed never to compromise his integrity again.

On 28 December 1944, just four days before his bills were due to be paid, he received an unexpected phone call. It was an offer for The Terrace. This was the only way out and he seized the opportunity with both hands. He felt a huge burden had been lifted off his shoulders. He could clear his debts and still have money left over.

He was convinced the business had crumbled because of his unfaithfulness to God but now he felt forgiven and restored. He had learned his lesson and although it had been very painful, he thanked God for it: 'By this He turned me back into the path of His direction in my life. I have found out that God loves me. And all God does is for my own good.'

Fruit gift boxes

In the very week that The Terrace was sold, Anthony embarked on yet another venture. Believing he could make a commercial success of packaging quality fruit in attractive gift boxes and selling them at bargain prices, he looked for premises in Miami.

Remarkably, considering it was wartime, he very quickly found an available empty store on busy Flagler Street in the heart of the shopping centre. He attributed this directly to God's guidance as store space was at a premium, especially in such a prime location as Flagler Street.

Anthony scoured Miami's supermarkets in search of the finest fruit, carefully choosing each individual orange and grapefruit to ensure that it was good enough for his gift boxes. Florence's niece Dorothy Brown and her husband Bob, who had moved to Miami, joined him in his new enterprise and with their help he developed a thriving business. People were soon talking about the quality of the fruit, the careful and tasteful packaging and the low prices. Sales boomed. The reputation of the gift boxes spread beyond the State and eventually large stores such as Macy's in New York City began to stock them.

After three years of continual growth, Anthony decided to cut out the supermarkets from which he obtained his fruit supplies and buy directly from the growers. This would reduce his costs (currently $2.50 per box) and lower his sale price (currently $5.50 per box), thus attracting more customers and increasing turnover. But to buy in bulk and avoid high transportation costs he had to be near the citrus groves. And so, in 1947, he and Florence took the decision to return to the Bradenton area, leaving Bob and Dorothy in charge of the store in Miami.

Launch of the Manatee River Packing Company

Anthony was sure God was leading him when he found just the site he needed on the very first day of his search. It was in Palmetto, just across the Manatee River from Bradenton. Situated next to a railway line and housed in a 200-foot-long warehouse fully equipped with machinery for sorting and washing fruit, the Overstreet Packing Company had been standing idle for two years. It was available for just $3,000. Anthony snapped it up and promptly launched the Manatee River Packing Company.

As soon as the plant was ready, work began processing the high volume of oranges and grapefruit that arrived daily in the warehouse. Just as Anthony had expected, his costs dropped dramatically. The $2.50 unit cost per box in Miami was now just 50 cents in Bradenton. He immediately reduced his sale price from $5.50 to $3.50 while maintaining the same profit margin of $3 as before.

The lower selling price had exactly the desired effect. Turnover rose astronomically and before long two railway wagons filled with gift boxes headed daily from Bradenton to destinations across the country.

A revolutionary idea

The careful selection of oranges and grapefruit for quality and size left Anthony with a major headache. What should he do with the fruit that was too small to be included in the gift boxes? He hit on an idea that was to revolutionize the industry.

Having lived in New York City, he knew that the famous Waldorf Astoria hotel served segments of orange and grapefruit as appetizers and in salads. Some forty women were employed full-time to slice the fruit into segments and to squeeze the oranges into juice. Anthony saw a market niche for his undersized fruit: he could produce ready-sliced orange and grapefruit segments and ready-squeezed orange juice.

But there was a major obstacle. While production would be easy, transportation would not. It was simply impossible, he was told, to prevent the fruit from spoiling on its thousand-mile journey from Florida to New York. He would have to find a way to keep the gallon jars in which the fruit segments and orange juice were contained chilled during the journey. Anthony prayed for an answer and it came.

The solution was simple. He would acquire a fleet of trailer trucks and blow chipped ice into the spaces around the individual jars. This would not only keep the jars chilled but also wedge them into place. A thick ice-covered canvas sheet would then be stretched across the load. Regular stops would be made on the journey to blow fresh ice onto the canvas to keep the temperature in the trailer at freezing point.

Anthony went ahead with his plans. He bought a trailer truck, acquired a refrigerated warehouse on an industrial park in New York City and made his first delivery. To his sheer delight, the idea worked. The fruit segments and juice were perfectly fresh on arrival without the use of preservatives. It was a sensational breakthrough.

Word quickly spread and demand for Anthony's products escalated. The Waldorf Astoria alone ordered a thousand jars of sliced citrus fruit a week. Some two thousand dairies began to add his fresh orange juice to their deliveries of milk and cheese. Anthony continually increased his fleet of trailer trucks but such was the demand that he never had enough.

Fruit Industries, Inc.

It was not just the fleet of trucks that was inadequate; the plant in Palmetto had also become too small. After two years it was time to find a new site. It was also time to change the name of the company as the gift box business had given way to fruit segment and orange juice production. In 1949, therefore, the Manatee River Packing Company became Fruit Industries, Inc.

A suitable site was found just across the river in Bradenton close to a convenient railway line. The plant was fitted out with long stainless steel counters where fifty women were employed to slice fruit into segments of just the right size and without seeds. Anthony himself had trained them how to do this. When ready, the fruit was carefully placed in jars, some containing just orange or grapefruit segments, others containing a mix of grapefruit, orange and pineapple arranged in layers and marketed as 'Fruit Salad'.

Tropicana is born

Anthony attributed all his success to God's guidance. He never took a decision without first praying about it and was confident that God would even listen to his requests that other people might consider trivial. One of these was for a more engaging name for his company. He was not happy with Fruit Industries, considering it bland, unimaginative and easily forgettable.

As had happened several times before—too often, he was sure, to be mere coincidence—the answer came quite suddenly. As he was driving down the north–south Florida highway one day in 1950, he prayed about a new name. Almost immediately he noticed a motel displaying the sign 'Tropicana Cabins' accompanied by a logo of a little Hawaiian girl in a grass skirt. The word 'Tropicana' and the image instantly connected with him. He was in no doubt that this was the answer to his prayer. When he arrived home, he asked Florence what she thought. She shared Anthony's conviction. That day the now-familiar company name was born.

The next step was a logo. Playing on the name 'Tropicana', a cartoon character called 'Tropic Ana' was created. She was depicted as a cute little Hawaiian girl in a grass skirt with a black pigtail and balancing a bowl of oranges on her head. The bowl prominently displayed the word Tropicana. This instantly recognizable logo was well received. The appealing name 'Tropic Ana' and the endearing image quickly helped establish the company's identity in the marketplace.

The death of Florence

Sadly, during this exciting period of development at Tropicana, Florence suffered with serious heart problems. Her condition gradually deteriorated and on 21 April 1951 she died at Bradenton's Larrabee Hospital following a fatal heart attack. Just moments before she died Anthony had been holding her hand as they said the words of the twenty-third psalm together.

He was devastated by her death. He had lost a loving companion who had supported him in everything he did and who faithfully stood by him during his times of failure. He was inconsolable and tried to bury his grief in long hours of hard work.

A crucial turning point

Immersing himself in work helped a little but Anthony found much greater comfort in the company of friends from church. They rallied round him with support, regularly coming to his home for Bible study and discussions on matters of faith. He found these times enormously helpful.

One of his friends had heard that an older lady was holding inspirational Bible study sessions in nearby Sarasota and had started to attend. This friend was so impressed by Mrs Northern's depth of understanding of the Bible, the clarity of her explanations and her lovely nature that one evening he invited Anthony to join him. It was to be a decisive turning point in Anthony's spiritual life.

He had come a long way in his understanding of the Christian faith and was grateful for God's guidance but his underlying unease remained.

Chapter 7

Although he had been stirred and given hope by the words of John 3:16 promising eternal life to those who put their trust in Christ, he could not claim that he felt their power.

During their conversation in the car on the way to the Bible study, Anthony's friend asked him if he was sure that he would go to heaven if he died that night. It was a question that still touched a raw nerve. Anthony's reply revealed his continuing uncertainty: 'How can anyone know that?'

The focus of the Bible study that evening was the very problem with which Anthony had been wrestling. The words of Romans 6:23 struck a chord with him: 'For the wages of sin is death; but the gift of God is eternal life through Jesus Christ our Lord' (KJV). They excited him but he still didn't know how to receive the gift. Mrs Northern went on to explain.

She told the group that everyone's sinful nature had been crucified with Christ on the cross. Just as everyone was included in His death, so they were included in His resurrection. Freed from the grip of their old nature, they could enjoy a new life—eternal life—united with Him. Sorrow for sin, a genuine desire for a change of heart and a willingness to receive Christ as Saviour were the sole requirements for peace with God and the assurance of heaven. No effort to please Him or impress Him was necessary. He accepted penitent sinners unconditionally.

Anthony was beginning to understand. As the Bible study continued, the message of Romans 8:1—'There is therefore now no condemnation to those who are in Christ Jesus'—struck him with the full force of a revelation. It was as if those words had been written just for him. He now knew in the very depth of his being that he was at last free from his fears of judgement and hell. Christ's death and resurrection guaranteed his place in heaven. A huge load dropped from him. 'My feet won't touch the ground for at least a week!' he joyfully exclaimed. From that time on he looked upon 1951 as the year he had been born again.

This was the start of a new direction in his spiritual journey. He no longer saw God as a judge who might send him to hell but as a close friend to whom he could entrust his life. He also saw Tropicana in a new light. It was now more than just a business; it was a vehicle to generate income to use in God's work. And as the company expanded, his giving increased accordingly.

Back to Messina

Anthony could not keep the good news of Jesus and the promise of eternal life to himself. He wanted his family and the people of Messina to hear the message and find for themselves the joy and peace that he had found. And so, in 1952, he paid a visit there.

The first person he wanted to talk to was his father, now eighty-one, but he was nervous as to how to approach the subject with him. He needn't have worried. His father not only listened intently but was inwardly moved. When Anthony thanked God at the lunch table for bringing the family safely together, his warm, sincere prayer brought tears to his father's eyes. It was obvious he had found faith.

Anthony's brothers and sisters, however, were not responsive. Each in turn thought of an excuse to get away when he tried to share his faith with them. He was disappointed but not disheartened and did not give up. Each September from 1952 he returned to Sicily to holiday with his family and in time they began to listen.

New HQ

Parallel with the growth in Anthony's spiritual life was the continual growth of his business. Its reputation for scrupulous honesty and the excellent treatment of its employees soon earned it the nickname 'the Christian orange juice company'. Anthony visited employees who were sick and in addition to other welfare benefits he provided a chaplain to offer help with any spiritual needs someone might have.

The company's reputation for quality products increased demand beyond the capacity of the plant to meet it and so, in 1953, relocation to a larger site became necessary. That year Anthony bought the former Florida Grapefruit Canning Plant in Bradenton to serve as his new HQ.

Just a year later, the newly erected cold storage building burst into flames. It was a horrifying sight. Huge plumes of black smoke rising from the massive structure were visible for miles around. The fire was put out before it could spread to other buildings but the damage was extensive, amounting to about half a million dollars. It was a major blow but surprisingly did not slow down the company's growth.

Chapter 7

Flash pasteurization

Anthony, ever creative, patented a pasteurization process that year which made it possible to store and transport pure orange juice without refrigeration. Called flash pasteurization, it substantially increased the distance over which citrus juice could travel. It also extended the shelf life of juice without loss of flavour, giving Tropicana a significant market edge over its competitors. Pure Premium, as this juice was called, became the company's flagship product.

Another first for the company was the production of a new form of packaging. Pure Premium orange juice became available in wax-coated paper cartons in half-pint, pint and quart sizes, making it much easier to sell to supermarkets and much easier for doorstep deliveries.

The S.S. *Tropicana*

With these and other developments, demand for Tropicana products escalated. It soon became impossible to supply the vast quantities of orange juice ordered by customers in New York and New England quickly enough. A million-dollar investment in expanding the fleet of trailer trucks made little difference. Somehow Anthony had to find another way of getting more juice to New York more quickly.

He was greatly exercised by the problem and could see no solution. As always when he needed guidance he turned to God in prayer. An idea soon came into his mind. He should use a ship. When he discussed this with others, they laughed. No one believed a huge cargo of orange juice could survive a two-and-a-half-day sea voyage without spoiling. It had never been attempted. Not surprisingly, in the face of such scepticism, Anthony did not find it easy to raise the $10 million he needed to finance the project. Banks dismissed his request for a loan. His frustration was understandable: 'When we made the first fruit section in jars, they think we are crazy. We start to chill juice, we are crazy. But the chilled juice got so good, we had to buy a ship to move it. That's crazy too.'

But he would not give up. Through dogged determination and sheer persistence he eventually found the necessary finance. Company profits provided some of the capital but, importantly, he was able to convince some more open-minded bankers of the compelling force of his calculations. He had been able to show them that the $265,000 cost of transporting 1,450,000 gallons of juice by truck to New York City would drop to a mere $15,000 if carried by ship, thus leaving a hugely increased profit margin.

With money now available, Anthony bought an 8,000-ton cargo ship for $650,000 from the United Fruit Company. Originally called the *Cape Avinov*, he renamed it the S.S. *Tropicana*. A suitable site was found at Port Canaveral on Florida's east coast to berth it and also to build a factory to process and store the juice.

There was much work to be done and Anthony wasted no time getting started. By February 1957 the nine buildings at the Port Canaveral plant had been completed at a cost of $5 million, the ship had been fitted out with six giant stainless steel tanks for the juice and a plant had been built on Long Island, New York City, to unload and package the cargo.

Anthony had given careful thought to the prevention of spoilage on the maiden voyage. The 1.45 million gallons of juice due for shipment had been stored as blocks of frozen ice before being ground to slush and piped directly into the ship's tanks. It was essential to maintain a constant temperature of 28°F in the tanks throughout the voyage. Anthony decided on lightweight high-strength foam glass, 6.5 inches thick, as insulation.

On 17 February 1957 the gleaming white S.S. *Tropicana* with its forty-two-man crew sailed out of Port Canaveral with its cargo. The occasion was marked with celebration and such was the interest in this milestone event that it attracted an international media presence.

Two and a half days later, on 19 February at exactly 1 p.m., the ship reached its destination on Long Island, enthusiastically welcomed by the 450 guests who had been invited to a celebratory banquet at the plant. The media were also out in full force. To the delight of all present the orange juice was perfectly fresh and its taste unimpaired. It was a landmark achievement and the first of countless shipments from Florida to New York. The technological breakthrough made Tropicana the world's largest producer and distributor of orange juice.

Just a year after the company's first successful shipment by sea, Anthony was elected 'Man of the Year' in Bradenton, an honour marked by the impression of his footprint in concrete on the pavement in front of the Court House.

Chapter 7

Marriage to Sanna Barlow

His amazing business success and the wealth that came with it gave him the opportunity to support causes close to his heart, especially Christian missions. Appropriately, then, he married a missionary—Sanna Barlow— on 11 September 1959 in London.

Sanna was born in 1917 in Johnson City, Tennessee. A committed Christian from an early age, she attended summer Bible camps for many years in her youth and later graduated in Biblical Education at Columbia Bible College (now Columbia International University) in South Carolina. She was also awarded a degree in teaching at East Tennessee State College, Johnson City. This was followed by the study of linguistics at the University of Oklahoma's Wycliffe Center which was renowned for its work in translating the Bible into many languages.

Sanna was a schoolteacher for several years but when she applied to become a missionary she was turned down because of her severe asthma. In 1948 she was employed by Gospel Recordings Inc. to record Bible texts in regional dialects in South-East Asia, South Africa and elsewhere. Her brother explained: 'They wanted to get all of the dialects in the world, so she just immersed herself in that kind of work. That became her missionary work.' She was also the author of several inspirational devotional books.

Anthony and Sanna married in London as it was a convenient departure point for their visit to Anthony's family in Messina.

Sanna was a great support to Anthony in his various activities. She enthusiastically participated in his annual Bible studies with his family in Messina and she played an active part at Tropicana. She frequently wrote speeches for her husband and was an excellent hostess when entertaining business colleagues.

The Mexican Pride

Despite Tropicana's phenomenal growth, things did not always go smoothly for the company. In December 1963 more than a third of Florida's orange crop was wiped out by a severe freeze. This was a disaster for the business and unless alternative sources of supply could be found, production the following year would be crippled.

Anthony felt that the way out of the crisis was to get his supplies from

Mexico where oranges were plentiful. He established a base at Tuxpan, a port in the Gulf of Mexico, from where he shipped cargoes to Florida. All went well until a Florida State inspector detected the presence of Mexican fruit fly on the third cargo and refused entry into the United States.

But difficulties always seemed to bring out the best in Anthony. He found a solution that surprised everyone. If the oranges themselves could not be brought into the country, their juice could. He came up with the idea of the world's first floating orange juice factory.

He bought a fifty-foot-wide old barge berthed at Port Sutton, four miles south of Tampa. It looked a sorry sight and was in need of a radical overhaul but after just three months it had been transformed into a seaworthy processing plant capable of holding 225,000 gallons of fresh orange juice. It was duly named *The Mexican Pride*.

But there was yet another obstacle to overcome. A busy highway blocked access to the dock in Tuxpan. How could the huge loads of oranges be taken across? Once again, Anthony came up with the answer: dig a tunnel under the highway and shunt the oranges through it directly onto the ship.

Processing began in the final week of March 1964 and immediately the media were captivated. Nothing like this had been seen before and headlines appeared in praise of 'the first floating factory of its kind'. It was another first for the company. *The Mexican Pride* served Tropicana well until normal supplies of oranges in Florida were once again available.

Mission to Messina

Inevitably the runaway success of Tropicana products in the USA led to exports to markets overseas. In 1966 fresh orange juice was exported to Europe for the first time when 14,000 cases of juice in glass bottles were shipped to France.

But in the summer of 1966 Anthony looked towards Europe for another reason. His sights were very firmly set on Messina. On visits to his family during the past few years, he and Sanna had been increasingly encouraged by the positive response to their Bible studies. Not only family members but their friends, too, had begun to attend. Anthony was now convinced it was time to tell a wider audience about his discovery of the love of God in Christ. To this end he planned to hold a five-day series of evangelistic meetings in the town. He enlisted the help of his brother, Alfredo, who lived in Messina, to publicize the meetings and find a suitable venue. He asked his nephew, Ralph Nicosia, who was working for Tropicana in the USA, to fly to Messina to help with the final preparations in the seven weeks leading up to the crusade.

There were many problems. The only available venue that Alfredo could find was hardly favourable. It was not conveniently located, it had no air conditioning and there was no lift to the floor where the meetings would take place. Furthermore, Ralph was alarmed when he met with all the pastors in the town and discovered that several of them had fallen out with each other. They were unlikely to cooperate in the venture. Things did not look promising but Anthony was not dismayed. He told Ralph, who had kept him abreast of developments: 'The Lord has put it in our hearts to preach the gospel. Continue to make the arrangements.'

Ralph continues the story:

> We had prayed and prepared and were trusting the Lord to do the rest. In spite of the location and other hindrances we had people come each evening. At the end of each message, my uncle gave the invitation to come forward to accept the Lord Jesus as Savior and we were amazed at the work of the Holy Spirit each evening. At the end of the crusade, a Brethren pastor who had displayed a humble spirit and love for the Lord and for His Word, Brother Osvaldo Lagana, was asked to shepherd the new converts. He gladly did. That was the birth of the Chiesa Biblica Cristiana [The Christian Bible Church].

This church has gone from strength to strength over the years and continues in Messina today.

Tropicana goes public

The growth of the church in Messina would have given Anthony great joy. So, too, would Tropicana's rapidly increasing market strength. By 1969 its turnover had more than doubled over a five-year period to $68.4 million. That year it gained a listing on the New York Stock Exchange and went public. The infusion of new capital from its stock offering was the platform for a further growth spurt.

The Great White Juice Train

In 1970 Tropicana was at the forefront of yet another technological development. As the demand for its fresh orange juice and grapefruit juice continued to soar, transportation couldn't keep up with production. The S.S. *Tropicana* was no longer adequate and had already been phased out. Other methods of transportation such as piggy-back trailers on railroads had been tried but to no avail.

It was the president of the Seaboard Coast Line Railroad who suggested that specially designed refrigerated boxcars (freight wagons) were the answer. Anthony embraced the idea and construction plans went ahead. They came to fruition on 1 June. That day two engines pulling sixty boxcars loaded with one million gallons of bottled orange juice pulled out of Bradenton on the start of their thirty-six-hour journey to a distribution centre in Kearny, New Jersey. The mile-long train with its white-painted wagons presented an impressive sight as it wound its way along the 1,250-mile route, It was given the nickname 'The Great White Juice Train'.

The impact on business was phenomenal. By the end of the year demand had reached record levels and net profits had soared by 85.2 per cent. The following year, 1971, two sixty-car trains were running weekly and before long a further hundred cars were added to the fleet. It was estimated that the saving in Tropicana's fuel costs during the first ten years of the juice train's operation was some $40 million.

The Golden Plate Award

Tropicana took a further step forward in 1972 when it opened its own corrugated box-making plant to lessen its dependence on outside suppliers. It was another example of Anthony's vision and dynamic leadership.

That year his accomplishments were nationally recognized by the American Academy of Achievement when he received the Golden Plate Award at a ceremony in Salt Lake City. This prestigious honour was awarded to 'men and women of exceptional accomplishment in the sciences, the professions, business, industry, arts, literature, sports, entertainment, and public service'. Anthony was publicly acclaimed at the ceremony as one of the USA's 'visionaries and achievers'.

Just a year later, in 1973, Tropicana opened a new processing plant at Fort Pierce on the west coast of Florida and by the end of the year turnover had reached a record $121.2 million. There seemed to be no end to Anthony's achievements as a businessman.

Chapter 7

Dinner at the White House

Perhaps the greatest honour that he received was an invitation to the White House. It was wholly unexpected.

On 1 February 1973 President Nixon had arranged a dinner in honour of Sir Edward Heath, Prime Minister of the UK. Top political figures from the USA and UK were present for the glittering occasion marked with great pomp and ceremony. But Anthony was puzzled. The invitation card had not made it clear why he had been made invited.

What a surprise when he found out why! He was one of a very select group of people introduced by the President as 'the 110 most important people in America tonight'.

More honours

Awards kept coming. In 1975 he received the Freedom Foundation Award honouring Americans 'who set examples in responsible citizenship, free enterprise education, and long-term civic accomplishment'. Two years later he was inducted into the Florida Citrus Hall of Fame in recognition of his 'significant contributions to the Florida citrus industry'.

Anthony's personal honours and Tropicana's astronomical growth continued hand in hand. By 1977 the company had won new markets in the USA, was exporting to several countries in Europe and was operating in the Bahamas, Bermuda and the West Indies. Profits had doubled every two and a half years during the previous ten and by the end of 1977 turnover had reached $244.6 million.

The sale of Tropicana

Not surprisingly, Tropicana's staggering success attracted the attention of many hopeful buyers but Anthony continually turned them away. At the age of seventy-seven he was as sharp as ever and still actively involved as chairman, CEO and president and keeping a close eye on every aspect of the business. As he had done for years, he continued to sample the orange juice on a daily basis to ensure its quality and taste were right.

But in his heart of hearts he knew he could not continue indefinitely and would have to retire some time. He felt that time had arrived in 1978. In August of that year, after much thought and prayer, he agreed a sale of almost $500 million to Beatrice Foods, a company for which he had the greatest respect. He was at peace with his decision.

Retirement
Anthony found retirement difficult at first. It was an emotional wrench to leave the organization he had built from nothing to become the largest chilled orange juice company in the world. But the close of one career was to become the doorway to another.

With the capital from his share of the sale of Tropicana and with plenty of free time, he now had the opportunity to serve God in new and exciting ways. To this end, he established the Aurora Foundation to provide funding for Christian educational institutions, Christian missions and numerous charities worldwide. He also founded the Bible Alliance to provide blind persons and prison inmates with cassette recordings of the Bible and of Christian messages.

In a birthday speech several years into retirement he summarized the contrasting nature of his business and current work: 'In Tropicana, I had the pleasure of providing orange juice, a product healthful for the physical life. But today, mine is the greater pleasure to be providing that which can bring health to the soul.'

Honorary doctorate
Although he was no longer active as a businessman, Anthony's astonishing achievements were not forgotten. With no more than the equivalent of a high- school education he had taught himself mathematics and mechanical engineering to such a high level that he was able to invent and patent equipment that revolutionized the citrus juice industry. On 26 April 1980 he was awarded the honorary degree of Doctor of Humane Letters by the University of Tampa in recognition of all that he had accomplished.

In his address at the ceremony he outlined some of the principles that had guided him to success and he encouraged the audience to follow them. He urged them to have a clear purpose and goal and not to be discouraged when difficulties arose, to use knowledge wisely, to be honest and to treat colleagues and subordinates with care. He concluded with what he considered the most important piece of advice of all: 'Listen to God. Have faith in God. Let Him guide you.'

Chapter 7

The Bradenton Missionary Village

Long before the sale of Tropicana, Anthony had been very concerned for missionaries who had completed many years of active service and had nowhere to live on retirement. Now, in his own retirement, he had the chance to help them. He decided to build a village for them that provided comfortable, well-furnished and well-equipped accommodation in pleasant surroundings.

He found an ideal hundred-acre site eight miles east of Bradenton and promptly bought it. The first spade of earth was turned one morning in 1980 when he, Sanna and some friends dedicated the project to God and asked His blessing on it.

The Bradenton Missionary Village, when completed, was magnificent. It comprised over one hundred houses set in landscaped grounds with citrus trees, lakes, fountains and beautiful flower beds. 'This was just a miracle to have a provision like this,' said one grateful resident who had spent nearly fifty years as a missionary in Africa. 'You can't beat this anywhere in the world,' added her husband. Anthony had cut no corners in providing the retired missionary community with the best of everything.

'The Top Ten Most Generous Living Americans'

His generosity in building the village and supporting numerous other causes was featured in an article in *Town and Country Magazine* in December 1983 in which he was named as one of the top ten most generous living Americans. The following extract lists some of his beneficiaries:

> The Founder and former chairman of Tropicana Products converted to Baptist faith after coming to the United States from Sicily; since then he has spent millions to further the work of Bible schools and missionary services—including the funding of a church in his native Sicily. His Aurora Foundation built the Bradenton Missionary Village, a one-hundred-acre, $10 million Florida community for retired missionaries.

In addition to his large-scale generosity Anthony also gave truckloads of free orange juice to Christian colleges throughout the country and he provided free pineapples at Tropicana's main entrance for the benefit of local people.

Florida Agricultural Hall of Fame

In 1987 another honour came his way when he was inducted into the Florida Agricultural Hall of Fame at the Florida State Fair in Tampa.

The Hall of Fame was created to recognize the outstanding and lasting contributions of men and women to agriculture in Florida and to preserve the history of agriculture in the state.

Death and legacy

It was to be the last honour Anthony received. On 24 January 1993 he died in Bradenton at the age of ninety-two. His funeral service took place at Calvary Baptist Church, Bradenton, where he had worshipped for the last twenty-three years of his life and served as a deacon and Sunday school teacher. Following the service he was interred in the Manasota Memorial Park. His memory is preserved in Bradenton in the five-acre Anthony T. Rossi Waterfront Park bordering the scenic Manatee River.

Anthony had built a world-class business empire on principles of fairness and impeccable honesty, always personally ensuring that his products were of the finest quality. In addition, his support for Christian causes was proverbial, running into countless millions of dollars. But he always refused to see his wealth as his own. It was God's and he was merely the steward. He once declared: 'I will be ashamed at the judgement seat of Christ if I have one nickel that belongs to Anthony Rossi.'

When asked to look back over his life and extract from it the most important lesson we could learn to be more productive in our own lives, he replied: 'Know the difference between believing in God and trusting in God.' He would probably have regarded this as a suitable ending to the chapter.